BIPOLAR WORKBOOK

How to Live an Empowered Life With Bipolar

(Get the Life That You Deserve, Never Be Depressed Again!)

Kenneth Nagel

Published by Oliver Leish

Kenneth Nagel

All Rights Reserved

Bipolar Workbook: How to Live an Empowered Life With Bipolar (Get the Life That You Deserve, Never Be Depressed Again!)

ISBN 978-1-77485-093-0

All rights reserved. No part of this guide may be reproduced in any form without permission in writing from the publisher except in the case of brief quotations embodied in critical articles or reviews.

Legal & Disclaimer

The information contained in this book is not designed to replace or take the place of any form of medicine or professional medical advice. The information in this book has been provided for educational and entertainment purposes only.

The information contained in this book has been compiled from sources deemed reliable, and it is accurate to the best of the Author's knowledge; however, the Author cannot guarantee its accuracy and validity and cannot be held liable for any errors or omissions. Changes are periodically made to this book. You must consult your doctor or get professional medical advice before using any of the suggested remedies, techniques, or information in this book.

Upon using the information contained in this book, you agree to hold harmless the Author from and against any damages, costs, and expenses, including any legal fees potentially resulting from the application of any of the information provided by this guide. This disclaimer applies to any damages or injury caused by the use and application, whether directly or indirectly, of any advice or information presented, whether for breach of contract, tort, negligence, personal injury, criminal intent, or under any other cause of action.

You agree to accept all risks of using the information presented inside this book. You need to consult a professional medical practitioner in order to ensure you are both able and healthy enough to participate in this program.

Table of Contents

INTRODUCTION 1

CHAPTER 1: DIAGNOSING BIPOLAR DISORDER 4

CHAPTER 2: TYPES OF BIPOLAR DISORDER 18

CHAPTER 3: BIPOLAR DISORDER TREATMENT OPTIONS .. 25

CHAPTER 4: CAUSES OF BIPOLAR DISORDER 32

CHAPTER 5: SIGNS AND SYMPTOMS OF RECOGNIZING BORDERLINE PERSONALITY DISORDER 37

CHAPTER 6: CONDITIONS THAT OCCUR WITH BIPOLAR DISORDER AND ITS COMPLICATIONS 66

CHAPTER 7: SELF-HELP AND TREATMENT 70

CHAPTER 8: HOW IS BIPOLAR DISORDER DIAGNOSED? ... 83

CHAPTER 9: DEPRESSION: WHAT IT IS AND HOW TO SPOT IT 99

CHAPTER 10: LIFESTYLE CHANGES AND HOME REMEDIES 102

CHAPTER 11: MANIA AND HYPOMANIA 106

CHAPTER 12: PROTECT YOUR PSYCHOLOGY 114

CHAPTER 13: TYPES OF BIPOLAR THERAPY 120

CHAPTER 14: LEARN HOW TO DEAL WITH THE THINGS THAT WILL STRESS YOUR MIND OUT 127

CHAPTER 15: TECHNIQUES TO LOWER YOUR STRESS 133

CHAPTER 16: TAKING ACCOUNTABILITY 139

CHAPTER 17: CHRONOTHERAPY, SLEEP DEPRIVATION AND MELATONIN 144

CHAPTER 18: WHAT IS THE WORST PART OF HAVING BORDERLINE PERSONALITY DISORDER? 151

CHAPTER 19: EXERCISE AND LIGHT THERAPY 172

CHAPTER 20: MAINTAINING A HEALTHY LIFESTYLE 178

CONCLUSION 187

Introduction

Bipolar disorder is one of the most complex and misunderstood illnesses in mental health conditions. There are so many cases of bipolar disorder that affect millions of people. Many also do not receive treatment, because they do not get the right diagnosis and thus cannot get the care that they need. As a result, we have mental health crises everywhere with people afraid of seeking treatment and quietly suffering from it or people who are living with the diagnosis and struggling to live their lives. But how does one expect to be able to live with this disorder? There has to be a way. There must be a solution to coping with this challenging illness. That's where this book comes in. We want to help. We want to show you how you can live a life with bipolar disorder that is successful and meaningful. Here is the breakdown of what you can expect from reading this book:

What Do You Expect to Get out of This Book?

1. To learn about the symptoms, diagnosis, and causes of bipolar disorder

2. To learn about treatment options with medication and psychotherapy

3. To understand how to manage the symptoms and live a productive life

4. To improve your wellness routine and maintain good overall health

This book is divided into eight concise and easy-to-read chapters that highlight how you can live a good life even while enduring the challenges of bipolar disorder. We will explain the illness in detail, treatment options that you can explore with your doctor and therapist, as well as tips that can help you learn to live with the stressors of bipolar disorder, which can continue even after a person as well. We will provide several case studies for you to understand how this illness works in everyday life. These are examples that you can follow in developing a treatment plan for you or your loved one, who is a patient of this illness. We hope that we can detail just how you can survive the storms of this illness, as well as experience victories that will last a lifetime. This is your guide to living with bipolar disorder.

Chapter 1: Diagnosing Bipolar Disorder

Although bipolar disorder is not as widely known or understood as other psychological disorders, it is by no means lesser in terms of its effects and symptoms. On the extreme, manic-depressive episodes can cause people to do things they don't normally do, especially if these episodes are coupled with bouts of hallucination and delusions. An untreated, undiagnosed bipolar patient might inflict harm on others as well as himself during manic-depressive attacks.

The only difference between bipolar disorder and other strands of psychological disorders is that the former is deemed more curable and controllable, as long as a patient is properly diagnosed and monitored. This is why, in most cases, diagnosis is vital for recovery and treatment of people with bipolar tendencies and symptoms.

The American Psychiatric Association (APA), along with other organizations, has devised several diagnostic instruments which aim to set a common language and reference for psychological conditions like bipolar disorder.

Diagnostic Instruments

Initial diagnosis of bipolar disorder relies heavily on a patient's reports and self-observations. It can be difficult to diagnose if a person is not aware that he is exhibiting some symptoms of mania and depression. After the patient's personal account, the next stage of diagnosis involves the observations of close family members and friends as well as the opinion of a psychiatrist or any other expert in the field of psychological disorders.

The main basis of the list of criteria for bipolar disorder in the US is APA's Diagnostic and Statistical Manual of Mental Disorders, 4th edition (DSM-IV-TR). For Europe and other parts of the world, the World Health Organization (WHO) also has a diagnostic manual called the International Statistical Classification of Diseases and Related Health Problems, version 10.

Aside from psycho-social symptoms, diagnosis might also involve a basic physical exam to look for physical symptoms in a patient's central nervous system as well as hormonal balance that can increase the risk of bipolar disorder. It is also meant to rule out medical conditions whose symptoms are similar to that of bipolar disorder. Such conditions include but are not limited to hyperthyroidism, chronic disease, and sexually-transmitted diseases like syphilis and HIV.

Medical scans and imagery might also be performed to rule out epilepsy and brain trauma. Once all the other diseases have been ruled out, the next step is to correctly identify and classify the case with the use of a diagnostic scale which includes a list of criteria such as the bipolar spectrum scale.

Bipolar Spectrum Diagnostic Scale

Through this instrument, people with bipolar disorder are often classified into sub-categories of mood disorders that fall under the bipolar spectrum. These mood disorders are those that indicate either abnormally elevated or depressed moods. Here are some of the codes used by this nomenclature to denote the prevalent points of the bipolar spectrum scale under which a case is categorized:

M is used to denote a bipolar patient who exhibits symptoms of severe mania.

D is used to denote symptoms of unipolar or severe depression.

m is used to denote that a patient shows symptoms of mania on a lesser scale (also known as hypomania).

d is used to denote symptoms of mild depression.

These four codes can be used in conjunction with each other to indicate mixed symptoms that usually manifest in people with bipolar disorder. For instance, the code Md might refer to a bipolar patient who has extremely manic episodes coupled with symptoms of mild depression.

The ordering of the letter codes may also be based on the order in which the patient experiences each episode. With bipolar patients, unipolar depression or unipolar mania is very rare. More often than not, patients show underlying minor symptoms of depression or mania beneath a dominant or extreme symptom or episode.

This scheme is also used to identify other mood disorders that are related to bipolar disorder but not necessarily connected. Major depression (code D) is one of them, while experts also suspect that there is a large portion of the undiagnosed population who also experience hypomania (code m) from time to time.

DSM-IV-TR/ICD-10 Classification

Under the diagnostic tools created by the APA and the WHO, we can correctly identify four major sub-types of bipolar disorder. These sub-types are generally used to specify the frequency of the episodes and the type of episode that the patient experienced most recently.

The sub-type Bipolar I is used to refer to cases wherein the patient has experienced at least one or more than one manic episodes, or if the most recent episode was of the manic type. Under this sub-type, hypomanic and mild depressive episodes also usually occur although they are not required criteria for diagnosis. Manic episodes are usually accompanied by psychosis or if not, they cause a major hindrance in the patient's ability to attend to regular activities such as work and school.

The Bipolar II sub-type refers to cases wherein the patient has had no history of manic episodes but did have hypomanic as well as major depressive episodes. It's important to identify that hypomanic episodes do not go beyond the borderlines of an extreme manic episode, since manic episodes are mostly connected with Bipolar I. Many Bipolar II cases are often incorrectly identified as major or chronic depression because patients don't correctly identify and report the hypomanic episodes that they experience (though this is through no fault of their own).

Cyclothymia is a milder version of Bipolar II which is often characterized by frequent hypomanic and depressive episodes that don't qualify as crippling, major depressive episodes. The term is derived from the regular low-grade mood cycle that for the patient seems like a part of his or her personality ("being moody") instead of a symptom of bipolar disorder. These mood cycles are usually identifiable because they still obstruct the patient from functioning properly at times.

Bipolar NOS stands for bipolar cases not otherwise specified. It is used to refer to cases when a patient shows multiple or mixed symptoms of one or more of the sub-types mentioned above or when he shows a mix of symptoms that do not fit into any other sub-type.

Episode Frequency

On average, people with bipolar disorder may experience at least 0.4 to 0.7 episodes of abnormal mood levels (mania, hypomania, or depression) annually. Each episode may last any period of time from three to six months.

A majority of diagnosed bipolars, however, are also diagnosed with rapid cycling wherein they experience at least four major episodes annually. Some patients even experience rapid cycling of moods within a span of several days or sometimes even within the day (known as ultra-rapid cycling).

Related Disorders

The symptoms mentioned in the previous chapter and the mood cycles in the bipolar spectrum are not exclusively identified with bipolar disorder. In fact, there are several psychological conditions which may have similar symptoms. Here are just some of them and their differences with bipolar disorder.

Schizophrenia refers to a psychiatric condition wherein a person experiences thought disturbances as well as the inability to generate emotional responses. The most common symptoms associated with this disorder include auditory hallucinations ("hearing voices"), paranoia, and delusions. Bipolar patients who experience extreme episodes of mania or depression might be mistaken as schizophrenics.

Dissociative Identity or Multiple Personality Disorder is a very rare psychiatric condition wherein a person's behaviour is alternately controlled by two or more separate and distinct identities. The existence of these multiple personalities goes unchecked because patients often experience memory impairment when the switch of personalities occurs. It is not a condition induced by substance use. It's also extremely difficult to diagnose because this disorder is often accompanied by other psychological disorders. Bipolar patients might show similar symptoms, especially since they experience two opposite extremes in terms of mood and energy levels.

Borderline Personality Disorder is a psychological disorder often characterized by excessive and unstable emotions, impulsiveness, and self-esteem. People with BPD are extremely paranoid of getting emotionally hurt or abandoned by the people they love, and some might also show patterns of suicidal tendencies and inflicting hurt upon themselves.

Attention Deficit Hyperactive Disorder is a psychological disorder distinguished by problems in a person's attention span, impulsivity, or even hyperactivity that are not considered normal. ADHD is usually diagnosed in children between 6 and 12 years of age. The hyperactivity of people with ADHD might be similar to manic or hypomanic episodes of people with bipolar disorder.

Bipolar disorder can lead to the development of other psychiatric disorders as a form of complication if it is left untreated. Aside from the disorders mentioned above, other conditions which may coexist with bipolar disorder are panic disorders and obsessive-compulsive disorder.

Famous Bipolar Individuals

Bipolars are different from psychopaths or any other individuals who have antisocial tendencies. Although some bipolars might commit crimes at the height of a hallucinatory episode, a lot more are actually high-functioning individuals who are considered experts and prodigies in their field. Psychological experts suggest that high-functioning ability is actually connected to hypomanic episodes.

Some bipolar individuals whom you might recognize or even idolize are Ludwig Van Beethoven, Amy Winehouse, Edgar Allan Poe, Florence Nightingale, Catherine Zeta-Jones, Vincent Van Gogh, Sidney Sheldon, Mel Gibson, Frank Sinatra, Virginia Woolf, and Jean-Claude Van Damme.

Chapter 2: Types Of Bipolar Disorder

Different people undergo varying patterns of episodes which determine their exact type of bipolar disorder, and the dominant patterns outlined in DSM-IV are bipolar I and bipolar II disorder. Other categories are cyclothymic disorder and bipolar disorder not otherwise specified (NOS). These patterns may or may not be accompanied with other features, like rapid cycling or psychotic symptoms. The severity of the symptoms varies in the same person over time and widely between individuals.

The major forms of bipolar disorder are:

Bipolar I: This type is diagnosed when the individual has experienced at least one full manic episode. Regardless of whether the individual may not have displayed any clinical depression and may have experienced past episodes of hypomania, whenever a full manic episode occurs, the individual is automatically diagnosed with bipolar I.

Bipolar II: This type is diagnosed when the individual has displayed only formal hypomanic episodes. The individual may or may not have displayed episodes of depression, but they have never displayed a full manic episode.

Cyclothymic Disorder - Cyclothymia is a pattern that involves hypomanic and mild depressive symptoms that have been experienced for two years or more. The symptoms of cyclothymic disorder, though milder than bipolar I or II, are however still severe enough to cause problems and difficulties in everyday life. Cyclothymia and bipolar disorder exist on a continuum.

Bipolar disorder NOS - Bipolar disorder NOS is a diagnosis of episodes that do not last long enough to be categorized as hypomanic, manic, mixed or major depressive episodes, or episodes without the required number of symptoms. There is some controversy about if particular temperaments should be categorized as bipolar disorder NOS, or further subdivide bipolar disorder on a continuum from its more severe to its milder forms. Some people may have temperaments that are initially similar to very mild bipolar symptoms and which may later grow into more established forms of bipolar disorder.

Hyperthymic: very cheerful, extroverted, optimistic, confident, and always busy

Cyclothymic: fluctuating mild mood switches, changing levels of self-esteem

Dysthymic: typically joyless, lacking in energy but not at levels as severe as depression

Depressive mixed: mild symptoms of anxiety, sadness, irritability, restlessness.

The Bipolar Spectrum - For individuals who have never experienced mania or hypomania, a unipolar illness diagnosis may be clear. Many people believe bipolar disorder is quite different from unipolar disorder, but in reality, the difference is not clear-cut. For instance, an individual may have predominant symptoms of depression and minor experiences of mood elevation that are too brief or mild to be categorized as bipolar disorder; however these symptoms are categorized into the bipolar spectrum and these individuals may indeed benefit from treatments usually used to treat bipolar disorder. Likewise, some individuals diagnosed with unipolar depression develop hypomania when they begin using antidepressant treatment. Although the boundaries of the spectrum are fluid and controversial, it is possible that about half of everybody who experiences diagnosed depression suffer from some type of bipolar disorder. Individuals with illness that falls into the bipolar spectrum have more potential to develop depression linked to marked fatigue, increased sleep, and to experience feelings of flatness, instead of sadness.

Rapid Cycling - Happens when you switch from one episode of illness, maybe depression, into another, e.g., mania or a mixed state. According to DSM-IV, rapid cycling is diagnosed when an individual has at least four episodes of illness, e.g., mania or depression, in one calendar year - but rapid cycling can happen more frequently than that, with some individuals cycling within weeks or even days. This condition is not rare, as it happens somewhere between 15 and 25 percent of people with bipolar disorder. The treatment for those with a pattern of rapid cycling greatly differs from the treatment for people without, so it is essential for you to recognize if this is your pattern. People with rapid cycling are more likely to be female and younger, or people who become ill later in life. They may have more episodes and hospitalizations. Antidepressants and thyroid problems may add to rapid cycling and although for some people, they cycle from depression to mania, their dominant experience is depression.

Seasonal Pattern - Some individuals discover that they typically have episodes at a certain time of the year. Personally, you may discover that you are more likely to have a major depressive episode in autumn or winter and/or a hypomanic or manic episode in summer or spring. Recognizing these patterns can help you find ways of reducing the severity of the episode or totally preventing it.

Chapter 3: Bipolar Disorder Treatment Options

Bipolar disorder may be a crippling mental ailment, but it is manageable. Do not lose hope if you have been diagnosed of having bipolar episodes, it is not the end of the world. With the help of certain medications and doing a couple of healthy lifestyle changes, you can significantly decrease the number of episodes you get and also reduce their intensity.

Medications for Bipolar Disorder

Once you have experienced more than two bipolar episodes, you are therefore required to take maintenance medications for the rest of your life, or for the long term at the very least. Fortunately, once your doctor has stabilized your mood swings using medications, you will be taking lower doses as time passes.

Lamotrigine and Lithium are two of the most prescribed, and most effective, medications that are prescribed for bipolar patients. Although these drugs can and will provide you with relief, they do have some side effects that you need to be aware of.

Lamotrigine

Lamictal (commercially-available Lamotrigine) is the most popular, FDA-approved maintenance medication for adults suffering from bipolar disorder. This drug can delay and decrease the intensity of the mood swings that accompany bipolar disorder, more specifically the bouts of extreme depression.

Lamictal's was originally meant to be a anti-convulsant, a form of medication that is meant to prevent or delay seizures when treating people with epilepsy. It was only recently that medical researchers found out that it has significant mood-altering and antidepressant effects that can be useful in treating bipolar disorder.

Side Effects of Lamotrigine (Lamictal)

Common side effects that come with the use of Lamictal include, but are not limited to:

- Headaches

- Diarrhea

- Blurry Vision and Dizziness

- Weird Dreams and Slight Hallucinations

In addition, around 3 out of 1000 people are allergic to Lamotrigine. If you find that you have developed a very itchy rash shortly after using Lamictal, you should discontinue using it and tell your doctor, because oftentimes they can be fatal.

Lithium

Lithium (available under the brand names Eskalith and Lithobid) has been used to treat bipolar disorder and depression for the longest time; it has actually been around for more than fifty years. Lithium was once only thought to minimize and decrease the instances of patients' manic episodes, but later it was found out that it can also be used to treat bipolar depression.

Lithium is used as a long-term or lifetime maintenance treatment for bipolar disorder. If you have started using lithium to manage the symptoms of your bipolar episodes you need to follow your doctor's advice and not stop the treatment on your own. Studies have shown that more than

90% of patients who went against the advice of their doctors and stopped taking lithium experienced relapse, and they are often much worse than before. Another drawback of stopping lithium use abruptly rather than gradually can decrease the effectiveness of the drug if you ever relapse and need to take it again to control your extreme mood swings.

Around 75% of patients who were prescribed with Lithium have been reported to experience side effects, albeit very minor ones that can be treated by lowering the dosage. It is not advisable for you to lower your dosage on your own once you experience side effects, you should always consult with your doctor first.

Here are some of the said side effects of taking Lithium:

- Abrupt Weight Gain

- Memory Problems

- Loss of Focus and Problem Concentrating

- Confusion and Mental Slowness

- Hair Loss

- Acne Breakouts

- Excessive Thirst and Cottonmouth

- Excessive Urination

- Blurry Vision and Dizziness

- Nausea, Vomiting, and/or Diarrhea

- Decreased Thyroid Functions (can be counteracted using hormone therapy)

Some of the more serious side effects include the weakening of bones in children and cause birth defects in 1 out of 1000 childbirths. Long term Lithium treatments can also impair liver and kidney function, which is why patients need to undergo blood tests every couple of months to inform their attending physicians if there are any serious repercussions that need to be dealt with.

If you are not keen with the idea of medication, you really do not have any choice at this point in time. You need to take your medication regularly if you want your bipolar episodes to stop; there are no ifs and buts about it. Hopefully, in the near future, scientific studies will be able to find a permanent cure for bipolar disorder, but as of right now, all you can do is take your prescription medicines and learn how to cope with what you are dealt with.

Chapter 4: Causes Of Bipolar Disorder

As with any other mental disorders, bipolar disorder can also be explained by several factors. Several studies were conducted in order to pinpoint what exactly causes this disorder. However, bipolar disorder cannot be explained by one factor alone. More often than not, a number of these different factors combine to explain the etiology of the disorder. Two most popular factors in explaining a mental disorder will be discussed in this section – the neurological factors and psychosocial factors.

There are many approaches used in understanding the neurological factors involved in bipolar disorders. One must keep in mind that neurological factors are anchored on the body's biology. Explanation regarding genes, the physiology of the brain, and chemicals found in brain are the core concepts to which neurological factors evolve.

First approach into explaining the neurological factors of bipolar disorder is genes. Studies show that bipolar disorder is the most heritable disorder. This means that if an individual's family has history of bipolar disorder, it is most likely that the individual will inherit the disorder. If an individual has either parents or even grandparents who were diagnosed of bipolar disorder, chances are that this person will also be diagnosed with the said mental illness.

The second approach into understanding neurological factors is the neurotransmitters. Our brain consists of chemicals that determine our mood, depending on the specific chemical's quantity. Serotonin, dopamine, and norepinephrine come into the picture. Any imbalance among the three hormones will likely cause disruption in the person's state of elation and depression. The shifts between states thus lead to hyperactivity during manic episodes and hypoactivity during depressive episodes.

Discovery in neuroimaging studies suggest that bipolar disorder is associated with the region of the brain involved in emotion. There are substantial changes in the activity in the said region of the brain. The changes are consistent with how emotionally reactive the person is. Studies show that bipolar disorder is related to increased activity in the region of the brain involving emotion, and to increased sensitivity of dopamine receptors, which influences the state of the brain.

Aside from the biological component that decides our makeup for vulnerability towards bipolar disorder, studies show that life events can also trigger bipolar disorder, particularly the depressive episodes. The depression in bipolar disorder is associated with low social support and poor social skills. For example, an individual may experience loss of a loved one. An individual who have low social support and poor social skills will not be likely to have someone to talk to about the grief that the person is experiencing, and will therefore delve into depression.

Mania, on the other hand, is psychologically explained by significant life events that trigger goal attainment. Sensitivity to reward is highly related to the vulnerability of demonstrating manic behavior. It is suggested that success on a certain pursuit trigger changes in confidence, which increases excessive goal pursuits. Aside from goal attainment, sleep is also seen as a factor contributing to bipolar disorder. The disruptions in sleep and circadian rhythms can trigger manic episodes. Currently, studies are not clear into establishing the reason why sleep deprivation is a contributing factor to mania. Nevertheless, studies have established that sleep deprivation is a major contributor to bipolar disorder.

Chapter 5: Signs And Symptoms Of Recognizing Borderline Personality Disorder

It is important that you are able to recognize the signs of borderline personality disorder so that the person who is suffering from it, whether it is you or someone else, is able to get the help that they need as soon as possible. It is really difficult to determine if someone has personality disorder like this one because they are often going to keep others far away. Those around them will just assume that the mood swings are because of a long day and they will often just think that the person has friends and family in another aspect of their lives rather than that the person is all on their own.

Recognizing some of the symptoms of personality disorder can really make it easier to help the person when they need it. We will get into more details about some of the specifics of these signs and symptoms, but basically, some of the symptoms you may notice with someone with borderline personality disorder include:

Lots of other mental health issues such as rage, substance abuse, anger, anxiety, and depression. You will find that when they are dealing with the borderline personality disorder, these underlying causes will sometimes make things a lot worse and without treating the depression or anger or other issue, they are not going to have a chance of getting better.

Impulsivity—they just want to get a thrill ride out of their lives and so they are going to do something that is fun and has a lot of risk. This is a way for them to get a little relief from their emotions, which they cannot control, for just a bit of time. The problem comes after the thrill is done thought. They are going to start feeling like they did something wrong and the guilt and worry are going to be worse than in the beginning. This can turn into a vicious cycle of trying to feel better without any results.

Self-damaging behavior—this might include things like cutting or burning themselves and could even include substance abuse. This is going to happen because the person with this disorder is going to put all of their feelings internally. They rarely if ever will hurt other people when they are upset or angry and instead they will do it to themselves. They may also do this because they do not think that they are worth anything and so

Concerns about being abandoned—people with this kind of personality disorder are always worried about being abandoned. Often this is their own doing though; they might get mad at the people who are trying to get close to them and cause them to go away or they may figure that they do not want to get hurt so they do not let anyone in.

Unstable self-esteem and relationships—pretty much, these kinds of people do not have any relationships and if they do, the relationships are not very strong and are not going to hurt this person if they end. They also have very low self-esteem.

Intense emotions that cannot be controlled—the person with borderline personality disorder is going to have a lot of issues with their emotions and they will not know how to control these emotions. Think about a young kid and how they are able to go back and forth between emotions in no time because they do not know the first thing about controlling them. This is the same thing that occurs with someone with this disorder.

A sense of identity that is very disturbed—they do not know who they are or what their purpose is. They may think that everyone hates them mostly because they do not understand how things work.

Chaos in their relationships—any relationships that are around are going to be a mess and probably will not last very long. For the most part, those who have this disorder are not going to have relationships that are good at all. They will have one for a short time that might be intense, but any little thing could set them off and they will get out of the relationship in no time. This is hard for others to be close to them because of this difficulty with their emotions.

These are just a few of the symptoms and signs that you will need to watch out for when it comes to dealing with someone with personality disorder. It is important to know all of these to determine if someone is going through this and needs some help. Some of the more intense side effects will be discussed in the following sections.

Emotional Symptoms

Let's take some time to look at the emotional symptoms that a person with this kind of disorder may have. People who are suffering from borderline personality disorder are the ones that are going to feel their emotions more than the others around them. They may feel them for a longer period of time, most deeply, and even more easily than other do. Also, these emotions are going to persist and come back over and over again. You may notice that the event to disturb them happened weeks ago, but the person is still suffering from some intense emotions because it will take them quite some time to get back to their emotional baseline and be stable again.

The emotions can go from one end of the spectrum to the other and they are not always about being sad, upset, or angry. Some people with this kind of disorder may be loving, joyful, idealistic, and enthusiastic, but at some times these may be to the extreme. Just because they can feel these positive emotions to an extreme does not mean that they are not going to become overwhelmed by all of the negative emotions that are surrounding them as well. For example, instead of feeling just sadness over an event they may feel some intense grief. They could feel humiliation and shame rather than just being a little embarrassed at a situation. Rage is often shown instead of annoyance and panic will show whenever they are nervous.

Often, these emotions are not totally out of the blue. There may be something that caused an emotion in the first place, but since these people are not able to recognize and control their emotions, the emotion is going to be blown way out of proportion. For example, instead of just being a bit embarrassed because you tripped going up on stage a bit, the person will feel like it is the end of the world and that everyone is laughing at them all of the time. In addition, instead of being just sad that their favorite show is over, they may hold onto this as intense grief for weeks to come.

People with this disorder are going to be really sensitive to what they perceive as their own failure, isolation, criticism, and being rejected. This is the person who at work you are just giving a suggestion to make things easier, not even really telling them they did anything wrong, and instead of taking it in stride and recognizing you are trying to help, they will overreact and think that you are telling them they have failed and are a horrible person. The emotion will go way out of proportion and they may hold onto this idea for a long period of time. The fact that they refuse to work with you and think that you are now against them is going to enhance their feeling of isolation because you really are not going to want to have anything to do with them.

Often the issues with them exhibiting suicidal behavior or causing themselves injury is due to the fact that the person with the disorder does not have any other way to cope with the things that are going on around them. They do not know that therapy, writing things in a diary, talking to others, or even living a healthy lifestyle will be able to help them to get through these emotions in a much safer and healthier way. Since they do not know this and their emotions are all over the place, they may feel like these two things are the only options that are available to them.

In some cases, the person with this disorder is going to be aware that their emotions are way off the grid and not acceptable to others, but they do not know how to control or regular these emotions. They then figure out that the best idea is to shut the emotions down all of the way. This is actually the part where a lot of people find out about the person suffering from borderline personality disorder since the negative emotions are going to alert others of the problem and they are going to work to address it.

Of course, there are times when a person with this kind of disorder is going to feel some intense joy in their lives, but since they are more prone to the feelings of dysphoria, or feelings of emotional and mental distress, this joy may not show itself very much. The dysphoria can make the situation worse because it heightens a lot of the issues that were already present in this person and makes them more pronounced. Those who are suffering from dysphoria may also experience feelings of being a victim, feeling of lacking an identity or being fragmented, being destructive to either themselves or to others, and going through extreme emotions.

While the person with this disorder is going to have emotional changeability, it is not the same as some others who are going through mood swings. Often these kinds of things imply that the person is going back and forth between being happy and then being sad. But with this kind of person, it often means that they are going to vary between anxiety and anger and then between anxiety and depression. While feelings of being happy can come about at times, usually the person is going to swing back and forth between these more negative feelings.

Behavior Symptoms

For those who are dealing with this disorder, it is not uncommon to have impulsive behavior. This would include things like reckless driving, reckless spending, having sex with multiple partners without using protection, eating disorders, alcohol abuse, and substance abuse. In addition, the impulsive behavior can start to go to other parts of the persons like such as self-injury, running away, and leaving out on relationships and jobs.

You may be wondering why a person with this kind of disorder would have anything to do with behavior of this kind. Basically it is a way for them to get some relief from the pain they are feeling from the emotions. These people are not able to control the emotions that they are feeling and often they will not understand why they are feeling emotions that are so intense. When they do the impulsive behavior, it gives them a nice rush, a moment of feeling better, and they begin to crave that moment to get a break from the crazy emotions that are boiling up in them.

It is important to note that even though this is used as a method of escape, in the long term these people are going to end up feeling more pain from their actions because they feel guilty and shameful for participating in them. This is a horrible cycle that is just going to make the person feel so much worse in the long run. In some cases, it may go on so long though that the impulsive behavior is done without thought when some kind of emotional pain comes to the person.

Self-harm

Many of those who are suffering from borderline personality disorder are going to have some issues with harming themselves or with suicidal behavior. In fact, this is one of the main criteria that will be used in helping to determine if a person actually has this kind of disorder or not. Management and then the subsequent recovery of this kind of behavior is going to be challenging and complex. There is always going to be a risk of suicide for the whole life of this person and the risk is somewhere between 3 percent and ten percent. While this might not be a high number of people who have committed suicide, many others with this condition will have thought about it in the past and may have attempted but did not succeed. There is also evidence that shows that men who are diagnosed with this condition are about twice as likely as women to commit suicide when they are diagnosed. There has also been some thoughts that many of the men who are thought to randomly commit suicide may have borderline personality disorder but they were not diagnosed.

Even if the person is not considering suicide or having these kinds of thoughts, it is still pretty common that they are going to perform some kind of self-injury to themselves. The reasons for the injuries are often different than the reasons for attempting suicide in most people. The reason for attempting to cause harm to themselves without trying to perform suicide are often to distract someone from their emotional pain, trying to generate normal feelings when they are feeling disassociated, as a form of punishment, and a way to express anger.

In contrast, when the person tries to commit suicide, they are showing thoughts that they believe that others would be better without them once the suicide is done. Both of these kinds of injuries are going to be the response of the person who is going through these negative emotions. They think that the abuse is going to let them feel normal or bring them back to reality and make things better, even though this is not the case.

One thing to note is that most of the people who have this disorder are usually not going to be able to cause any physical harm to those around them. Often this kind of personality disorder is going to be shown in the wrong light and many think that they are a bit crazy and could cause harm to those around them. Since most of those with this disorder have had abuse when they were younger, they are very against hurting others and any of the harm that they are going to do will be done to themselves rather to anyone else.

Interpersonal Relationships

Those who are dealing with this kind of disorder are often going to be really sensitive to the ways that others may be treating them. They may feel really intense gratitude and joy when they think that someone is treating them with a lot of kindness. On the other hand, they may feel some intense anger and sadness when they feel that someone else is criticizing or making them feel hurt. The feelings that they have about others is going to shift from one day or another and it will depend on the way that the person treats them, or at least the way that the person perceives they are being treated. They will often be worried about losing those they trust and they do not want to feel like they are going down in esteem from someone else.

This is a phenomenon that is known as black and white thinking or splitting and is going to include having a shift from idealizing others to devaluing them. The person does not see that things come in different colors and will only see them in black and white. For example, they may like someone at one moment and then may not like them or want anything to do with them because that person gave them a little criticism or didn't have enough time for them one time.

When this kind of thing is combined with devaluation, idealization, and the many mood disturbances that come with this disorder means that it is really hard for the person to have any relationships whether it is with their coworkers, friends, and family. Their own personal self-image is going to change from positive to negative very rapidly which can make them even more difficult to do deal with.

This can be really hard for the person who is suffering from the disorder because they really want to have some intimacy with those around them. Because they want the intimacy and are not getting it, they are more likely to be preoccupied with the attachment patterns in their relationships, they will feel insecure, and they may avoid other people. They may also see the world as a malevolent and dangerous place because they are not able to find the intimacy that they desire. The issue here is that they are often the ones who are keeping others at bay, even if someone wants to try and get with them.

In some cases of borderline personality disorder, the person may find that manipulation is the only way they are able to get the nurturing and intimacy that they would like. It is not that they want to be in control of the people who are near them though, like what is found in other mental illnesses. Rather, it is about trying to get someone to like them and they are not sure how else to do this process.

Sense of Self

One of the more noticeable things that others will say about someone who has this disorder. People with this disorder are going to have some trouble seeing who they are and they may see themselves as something much less. While others are going to see them as a great person who has gotten a lot of accomplishments and would be there to help anyone who needed it, the person is going to see themselves as worthless and someone that no one else would want to hang out with.

Often, these kinds of people are going to have a lot of difficulties with understanding that they have value and that others do really enjoy them when their emotions are not all over the place. In addition, they may often be unsure about their log terms goals whether it is for their life, jobs, or even relationships. This whole thing with not knowing who they are or the things that they value can make them feel more empty and lost.

Everyone has a time in their lives when they are going to feel like they are not sure of the goals that they want to reach in their lives. They may have just gotten out of school and were not able to get the job that they always wanted. Other times they may be worried about if they will be able to pay a bill or something else. It is normal to have times when the future is not so certain. But the person with this disorder is going to feel this way all of the time. They never have a plan for their life and they are always going to feel like they have no idea where they should be going.

It is pretty easy to tell if someone is having too much issues with their sense of self. These are usually people who are really good at what they can do, who might be the most loving and fun people to be around when they are dealing with their emotions the correct way, and they can be just as talented as others. But despite all of this, they are going to be very unsure of themselves and feel like they are not able to do anything write. They are going to go around believing that no one could possibly like them no matter what, and these feelings are not going to be because they feel like this is the way that they can get attention. Instead, they are doing it because they actually feel this way and nothing you do will convince them that this is the wrong way to think about themselves.

Cognitions

Finally, there are also going to be some cognition differences that occur in the person who is suffering from borderline personality disorder. Often the really intense emotions that these people will experience will make it really difficult for them to be able to control their attention and their focus. Often you will see that they are not able to concentrate on something for very long and they may spend a lot of time dissociating or zoning out during the day. Dissociation is an occurrence that is a response in some people when they are experiencing a somewhat painful event; or at least experiencing something that will make them remember that painful event.

During dissociation, the mind is going to automatically redirect the person's attention away from the painful event to protect them and make sure that some unwanted impulses do not happen. Although this is technically a way for the mind to block out these painful and intense emotions to provide some relief, in some cases it can block out even the good feelings that a person is experiencing and makes the person feel more numb. Those with this kind of disorder is going to find that it is impossible to make decisions because they do not have these normal emotions.

In some cases, it might be possible for an outsider to notice when the person with the disorder is dissociation, because the vocal and facial expressions can become expressionless or they may become flat and they will look distracted. Then again, there are times when it is impossible to tell when someone is going through dissociation at all.

This is a complex way of saying that the person with the disorder is not able to feel the emotions that are around them properly because their brains are not letting them. As mentioned before, a lot of the people who are dealing with this disorder have had something that was traumatic in their childhood. This could have been abuse, neglect, or the loss of someone who was close to them. Because of this bad experience, the person is going through dissociation about that event and if something reminds them of the event, they will go through the dissociation again.

While this might seem like it is a good way to protect the person, and most of the time when the process occurs that is exactly what is happening, when dissociation occurs too often, the person is going to be blocking out a lot of emotions that are a part of their daily life. They are going to miss out on joy, friendships, love, and happiness, as well as some of the bad things, because their mind is still trying to protect them and get them away from a situation that it thinks is harmful.

This could be used to describe why the person with borderline personality disorder reacts in this way. They are missing out on some of the emotions that are important to their lives and so they are not getting the full experience that is needed. Without that, they are not able to make the right decisions to make friends, get things done, or even think about their futures. They do not realize they are missing out on these emotions though so to them they are not seeing a problem at all.

Also, if the brain is forcing the person to go through dissociation when emotions start to come up, how is that person supposed to learn how to control all of their emotions? They might have these emotions come up randomly and they have to try and deal with them while other times the brain my try to take over instead. This is why many of those with this disorder are going to have a lot of trouble handling their emotions simply because they might not be as used to them as they should be.

Often therapy will look at this dissociation to figure out if it might be the issue behind some of the behavioral and emotional problems of this person. If the dissociation can be helped out, the person is going to be able to start learning about all of the emotions and learning how to deal with them rather than hiding. This process is going to be a slow one, but over time, they will learn what is going to work and that things are not as black and white as they have been used to seeing.

One of the only ways that you are going to be able to get help for this disorder is to get a diagnosis and treatment from a professional. The success rate for those who are able to go into treatment and stay for the required amount of time is the majority so it is really worth your time to go in and get the help. Asking for help can be difficult, but it is the only way to get control over the issue and get the best help possible. A professional will be able to diagnose this and make sure that the right questions and treatment are being offered to each client to get them to feel better.

These are just a few of the signs and symptoms of borderline personality disorder. It is important to understand these so that you are able to get the person the help that they need to stay healthy and get through the issues. Many people do not understand what is going on with this disorder so they will simply say that the person is crazy and should just get over it. But understanding where all of the behaviors and actions are coming from helps to show that the person is not actually able to control the way that they are acting and behaving.

Chapter 6: Conditions That Occur With Bipolar Disorder And Its Complications

A person who is diagnosed with bipolar disorder is also more likely to experience other conditions. When this happens, it is essential that you get the much needed treatment right away as any of the following conditions can only worse your condition. The conditions that occur if you have bipolar disorder include:

ADHD or the Attention-Deficiency Hyperactivity Disorder

There are cases where the signs and symptoms of people suffering from ADHD also known as the Attention-Deficiency Hyperactivity. This is basically the reason why sometimes it can be quite difficult to know if a person is suffering from bipolar disorder or from ADHD. In fact, there are also instances where a person might have both ADHD and bipolar disorder.

Anxiety Disorders

Having anxiety disorders can also increase your risk of developing bipolar disorder. For instance, if you have been suffering from post-traumatic stress disorder or if you have any phobia, these anxiety disorders can make your condition worse.

Health Problems

Most people who have bipolar disorder might also have problems with their health. If the person is obese, there is a higher risk of suffering from this condition. Other health problems include thyroid problems and heart diseases.

Addiction Abuse

Individuals who have addiction to certain substances are also at risk of worsening the problem. Many of those who are diagnosed with this condition are experiencing drug, cigarette or alcohol problems and abuse. Some people might think that drugs can remove the symptoms but in reality, drugs lead to worse bipolar episodes that can be really dangerous.

Complications of Bipolar Disorder

A person with bipolar disorder should get treatment right away. However, there are cases where in some individuals refuse to admit that they have it or others just would not seek professional help. If bipolar disorder is not treated, it will have serious and negative impacts in other aspects and areas of your life. The following are the complications that you might encounter if bipolar is left untreated:

Problems with personal and work relationships

Poor performance at work or school

The person may have suicidal tendencies

Prone to experience financial problems

Legal problems

Extreme loneliness

Substance abuse or addiction

Chapter 7: Self-Help And Treatment

Bipolar disorder can adversely affect the patient's quality of life. It can destroy relationships, limit career growth and opportunities, hinder excellent academic performance and may trigger suicidal attempts. However, this alarming condition can be managed and treatment is readily available such as medication and psychotherapy.

Request an appointment with a psychiatrist.

Bipolar disorder does not disappear on its own. The symptoms may worsen if untreated so it is a great decision to ask for help immediately. Before going to your appointment, list down all the details about yourself such as the symptoms that you've had, recent life changes, supplements that you are taking, and major challenges that you have encountered before the occurrence of the symptoms. These details would help the doctor diagnose your condition. If possible, it would be helpful if you can take a family member or a friend with you. Aside form the moral support that they can provide, they can also help you remember the things that the doctor have discussed. Ask questions. If you do not understand something, clarify it right away.

Give honest answers to the questions from your doctor.

The mental specialist will ask series of questions to screen if you are a potential candidate for bipolar disorder. The doctor may ask about the frequency and severity of your symptoms and when did they start. He may also ask questions about your family history and other mental and physical conditions that you have.

Undergo the required tests and exams.

When a doctor suspects that a patient has bipolar disorder, he performs a series of laboratory exams to validate the hypothesis. These include physical exam, blood test, psychological evaluation, and mood charting. Mood charting is the process of recording your daily moods that would help the doctor in coming up with an accurate diagnosis and treatment.

Understand that bipolar disorder requires a lifelong treatment.

The treatment will start with you taking medications to balance your moods immediately. Once the symptoms disappear, your doctor will give you maintenance treatment that will be used in managing bipolar disorder on a long-term basis. It is important to take your medicine regularly even during intervals when you feel better. Never miss a single dose. Skipping medications can precipitate a relapse. Medications include lithium, anticonvulsants, antipsychotics, antidepressants, symbax, and benzodiazepines.

Lithium- Lithium is also known as Lithobid and has been used as a bipolar treatment since the early years. It is very effective in regulating mood and preventing the occurrence of extreme highs and lows of some bipolar categories. However, lithium may cause kidney failures and thyroid issues so patients who are taking this medication are required to undergo regular blood tests.

Antidepressants- Your doctor may recommend you to take antidepressants if you manifest severe signs of depression.

But this medication has various side effects to patients such as reduced libido and problems in attaining orgasm during sexual activities. Antidepressants can also trigger manic episodes in some bipolar patients.

Anticonvulsants- These medications are effective mood stabilizers particularly for patients who has mixed bipolar episodes. Side effects may include drowsiness, skin blisters, liver problems, abnormal blood circulation and weight gain.

Antipsychotics- Antipsychotics are a good substitute for anticonvulsants. People who are not fit to take anticonvulsants can resort to these medications. Quetiapine is the only antipsychotic that was approved by the Food and Drug Association. There are also side effects that may vary from sleepiness, fast heart beat, blurred vision, and involuntary muscle movements.

Benzodiazepines- These medications help patients to have a better sleeping pattern and temporarily reduce anxiety levels. Benzodiazepines can cause memory disruptions, abnormal muscle coordination and drowsiness.

Symbax- Symbax is certified by the US Food and Drug Association and is approved as a medication for bipolar disorders. It is an effective treatment for depression and mood stabilizer. Weight gain, reduced sexual desire and increased appetite are the common side effects of symbax.

Your doctor will help you find the right medication for you however, since the full effects of some medications are seen after weeks or months, patients are required to have more patience during the treatment process.

Psychotherapy

Counseling is an essential part of the treatment process in bipolar disorder. There are various types of therapy that can help you manage bipolar symptoms.

Cognitive behavioral therapy- This is a usual form of individual therapy for bipolar patients. The goal of every session is to identify unhealthy, negative behaviors and mind-set then replaces it with healthy, positive ideas. This therapy will help you understand the causes of your bipolar episodes and provide you with effective techniques on how to handle and overcome these challenging situations.

Group Therapy- This is one of the most successful therapies for bipolar disorder that provides a forum so that patients can communicate with other people who are under the same mental situation. It provides a social avenue for patients and helps them establish better relationship skills.

Psychoeducation- This form of counseling is focused on helping patients to learn all the details about bipolar disorder. Being aware of the symptoms and what happens during bipolar episodes will help you recognize the warning signs and can do something before it leads to a full-blown bipolar episode.

Family Therapy- This kind of psychotherapy requires family members to be with the patient during doctor's visits.

Your doctor will conduct an evaluation and decide on the kind of therapy that may be appropriate for you.

Electroconvulsive therapy (ECT)

People who experience extreme depression and develop suicidal thoughts and have not improved despite other treatments can resort to electroconvulsive therapy. This therapy makes use of electrical currents that causes changes in the brain chemistry reducing the severity of the symptom. Pregnant women who can not take medications can use ECT as a bipolar treatment. This therapy can cause temporary amnesia and confusion.

Switch to a healthy lifestyle.

Bipolar treatment will be more successful if you make some healthy changes in your lifestyle that can help minimize bipolar episodes.

Stop smoking addiction and the use of addictive drugs. Drug abuse and excessive alcoholism is attributed to risky behaviors.

Build healthy relationships. Hang out with people who influence you in a better way and have the right attitude to inspire you to behave in an appropriate manner.

Stay active. Regular exercise can help stabilize your mood. When your muscles work, the body produces chemicals known as endorphins. These chemicals makes you feel good and help you sleep better.

Have an adequate sleep.

Sufficient sleep helps you manage your mood. The Sleep Foundation recommends at least 7-9 hours for adults in order for the body organs, especially the brain, to function properly.

Getting enough sleep is a common problem among adults. But you must try to have a good night sleep each night to avoid bipolar triggers.

Do not do in physical exercises three hours before you sleep. When muscles are active, the production of melatonin is suppressed that is a vital element in regulating sleep. It also awakens your system and this effect last for almost three hours making it more difficult for you to fall asleep.

Maintain a regular sleeping routine. Go to bed at the same time every night and wake up at the same time in the morning. Do not take afternoon naps or limit it to less than 15 minutes. Longer naps during the day will contribute to your inability to fall asleep at night.

9. Minimize stress.

Over thinking and numerous worries are powerful factors that often trigger depression episodes among bipolar patients. Try to relax your muscles by performing stretching routines and deep-breathing exercises. Stretching your muscles can help relieve muscle tension, give you comfort and calm your nerves.

Forget about your worries and do a series of inhale-exhale with your eyes closed. Slow, deep breathing lessens the effects of stress by maintaining your blood pressure in the normal level and decreasing heart rate.

Doing yoga and other mental exercises would also help minimize your stress levels. Focusing your vision on things that are green also delivers a calming effect to your brain.

10. Ask for support.

You do not need to undergo the difficult bipolar situation all by yourself. Accept that you have a mental condition that you can better manage with the help of the people around you. Let your family and friends know about your situation. You especially need their patience and understanding during the stages when bipolar episodes are its highest.

11. Have faith and do not give up.

As discussed in the previous page, bipolar treatment is a long process. Doctors will ask you to try different medications in order to find the right treatment for you. Read about bipolar patients who are now living a normal life and believe that you can be one of them. You just need to work for it by taking the proper care and treatment.

Chapter 8: How Is Bipolar Disorder Diagnosed?

Bipolar disorder is not easily diagnosed. Most of the time, it is mistaken for other problems including anxiety disorders, conduct disorders and/or mood disorders. Nonetheless, the enhanced understanding of mental disorders today paved a way in identifying the symptoms of bipolar disorder including mania, hypomania, and depression. It is important to note however that no laboratory tests or expensive imaging techniques can help in making an appropriate diagnosis. Instead, bipolar disorder can be identified through a series of open talks with a doctor about behaviors, mood changes and lifestyle practices.

History taking

A psychiatrist will ask about the symptoms a suspected bipolar individual experienced – the severity, length of time it lasted, when it first appeared and whether these manifestation were treated. Details regarding family and medical history will also be asked. Other family members will be interviewed if the suspected patient is a child or a teenager.

Psychological evaluation

The best person that will do the psychological evaluation is a psychiatrist. Diagnosis of bipolar disorder is based on the data gathered from history taking. This evaluation may include mental status exams to identify whether reasoning, interpersonal relationships, speech patterns and memory are affected which may possible occur on bipolar disorder. The psychiatrist may also evaluate the suspected patient for other mental health conditions to rule out other possible disorders.

Mood charting

The psychiatrist may ask the suspected bipolar patient to write down and keep a daily record of his sleep patterns, moods and other important factors that may help in diagnosing bipolar disorder.

Physical examination

A general practitioner will perform physical examination to help rule out physical causes of sudden mood shifts (e.g. hypothyroidism). Laboratory tests will be performed and if physical causes are ruled out, the suspected patient will be referred to a mental health professional for further assessment.

How is bipolar disorder treated?

Bipolar disorder can significantly impact an individual's life. It can lead to damaged relationships and career and may even result to suicide. To date, it has no cure but it can be treated. Proper treatment can greatly help in controlling mood shifts as well as the other manifestations. Treatment usually involves long-term psychotherapy and medication use to maintain a total control of the symptoms and prevent recurrence of manic and depressive episodes.

Medications

Medications used to treat bipolar disorder require prescription from mental health professionals including psychiatrists, psychiatric nurse specialists and clinical psychologists. It is important to note however that not all individuals respond to these medications similarly. One may need to try different medications before finding the best treatment. Keeping a daily record of moods, medication intake and side effects experienced will greatly help in monitoring the course of the illness as well as determine the most effective therapy for each patient. Some of the most common medications and its side effects are listed below.

Lithium

Lithium, more commonly known by its brand names Lithobid and Eskalith is the most commonly used medication for treating bipolar disorder. Earlier and recent studies regarding the efficiency of this drug show that it can greatly help in reducing the frequency and severity of manic episodes. It may also help in treating depression and may as well decrease suicidal tendencies. Lithium also helps in preventing recurrence of future mood shifts; hence, it is typically prescribed as a maintenance therapy for long periods of time.

Side effects:

Most people who take lithium to treat bipolar disorder experience some minor side effects. These are very apparent on the first few weeks of taking the drug. Oftentimes, these side effects are relieved through drug dose manipulation. One should take note however that it is important to consult the doctor before doing anything about the drug prescription. Common side effects of lithium includes hand tremors, thirstiness, frequent urination, weight gain, diarrhea, acne, fatigue, vomiting, memory problems, difficulty concentrating, hair loss and lethargy. Immediately notify your doctor if you experience slurred speech, diarrhea, fever, unsteady gait, fainting, rapid heartbeat and confusion.

Caution:

Pregnant women and breastfeeding mothers should not use lithium. Individuals with kidney problems, cancer, allergies, epilepsy and heart disease should also refrain from using lithium.

Anticonvulsants

Individuals who do not respond to lithium are prescribed with anticonvulsants. It helps in preventing and treating mood shifts through calming the hyperactive brain. Effective anticonvulsants include divalproex sodium/valproic acid (Depakene, Depakote), carbamazepine (Tegretol) and lamotrigine (Lamictal). This particular medication is prescribed for individuals who have rapid cycling bipolar disorder.

Side effects:

Most common side effects of anticonvulsants include drowsiness, fatigue, nausea, tremors, rash, weight gain and dizziness. These effects diminish over time.

Caution:

Pregnant women should consult their doctor before taking anticonvulsants. It can also cause serious liver problems upon prolonged use. Some anticonvulsants may interact with other medications such as aspirin and cause serious problems.

Antipsychotic medications

Antipsychotic medications are typically used as a short-term medication to control manic symptoms in bipolar disorder. Some antipsychotics can be used to prevent future bipolar episodes. However, it is often used to decrease manic symptoms including impulsive and reckless behaviors until mood stabilizers take full effect. Antipsychotics used for bipolar disorder includes aripiprazole (Abilify), clozapine (Clozaril), risperidone (Risperdal), lurasidone (Latuda), asenapine (Saphris), quetiapine (Seroquel), olanzapine (Zyprexa) and ziprasiodone (Geodon).

Side effects:

Some antipsychotic drugs used for treating bipolar disorder may lead to high cholesterol levels, weight gain and may even increase diabetes risks. Most common side effects include drowsiness, tremors, dry mouth and blurry vision. Older antipsychotic drugs are not often used to treat bipolar disorder as these drugs can cause a serious side effect known as tardive dyskinesia. Tardive dyskinesia is characterized by grimacing, lip smacking and protruding tongue.

Caution:

Individuals with heart disease and diabetes should take caution in taking antipsychotic drugs.

Antidepressant medications

There are different types of antidepressant used in treating bipolar depression. These include selective serotonin reuptake inhibitors (SSRIs), monoamine oxidase inhibitors (MAOIs), serotonin/norepinephrine reuptake inhibitors (SNRIs) and tricyclic antidepressants. Doctors however need to try out several of these antidepressants before arriving on a certain drug that will work on a particular individual. Antidepressants are usually used together with lithium and other medications to control bipolar symptoms.

SSRIs commonly used for treating bipolar depression include paroxetine (Paxil), fluoxetine (Prozac), fluzamine (Fluvox), sertraline (Zoloft), escitalopram (Lexapro), citalopram (Celexa) and vilazodone (Viibryd). MAOIs on the other hand include phenelzine (Nardil), tranylcypromine (Parnate), isocarboxazid (Marplan) and selegiline (Emsam). Atypical antidepressants include olanzapine and quetiapine. Antidepressants does not work immediately, individuals with bipolar disorder may need to wait for several weeks before experiencing its full effects.

Side effects:

Side effects of the different types of antidepressants are varying nevertheless; the most common one includes sleeping problems, weight gain or loss, decreased libido and dry mouth.

Caution:

It is important to closely monitor young individuals treated with antidepressants, as suicidal risks tend to increase with this medication. Individuals taking MAOIs should also follow a special diet to prevent serious complications.

Benzodiazepines

Benzodiazepines are used to control manic episodes in combination with mood stabilizers. It is taken for two weeks or less to restore an individual's normal sleeping patterns. Benzodiazepines that can be used to treat bipolar disorder includes lorazepam (Ativan), clonazepam (Klonopin), diazepam (Valium) and alprazolam (Zanax).

Side effects:

Benzodiazepines are fast acting medications which can sometimes lead to slurred speech, unsteady gait and dizziness. Other side effects also include memory loss, muscle weakness, blurred vision, fatigue and drowsiness.

Caution:

Benzodiazepines can be addictive. It shouldn't be taken with alcohol or any other medication without consulting the doctor. Taper off benzodiazepine use to avoid sudden withdrawal symptoms.

Psychotherapy

Psychotherapy or talk therapy is one of the most effective treatments for bipolar disorder. It can help a bipolar patient in managing relationships, stress, moods and uncomfortable feelings. It can also help in providing support and guidance not only to the patient but also to the family.

Researches reveal that there are some types of psychotherapy treatments effective for improving bipolar symptoms, which include:

Cognitive behavioral therapy

Cognitive behavioral therapy is a type of psychotherapy intended for individual treatment. It focuses in identifying negative and unhealthy behaviors/beliefs and replacing them with positive and healthy ones. It helps in identifying the triggers of bipolar episodes whilst teach bipolar individuals how to manage upsetting circumstances and stress.

Psychoeducation

Psychoeducation teaches individuals with bipolar disorder about the course of the illness and its treatments. It helps in educating people how to recognize the warning signs and relapses of impending bipolar episodes. Through recognizing these signs, support and care can be immediately sought.

Family focused therapy

Family focused therapy involves family members. This will help in improving the coping abilities of the members of the family. It will also aide in enhancing the family's ability to recognize early symptoms. This can help in improving interpersonal relationships, communication and problem-solving abilities of everyone in times of extreme mood changes.

Group therapy

Group therapy helps in providing a forum where everyone can share similar experiences and learn from each other. It also helps in building better relationship skills overtime.

Interpersonal and social rhythm therapy

Interpersonal and social rhythm therapy helps in identifying and resolving problems on one's daily activities. Following a daily sleep pattern and schedule can contribute in preventing manic periods.

Chapter 9: Depression: What It Is And How To Spot It

Another emotional state is depression, or a depressive episode, and these are no less severe than the manic phase. Depressive episodes are characterized by significantly low mood levels, and the persistent feeling of general gloominess or hopelessness. Individuals have described depression and depressive episodes as feeling burnt out, exhausted, and slowed down.

These episodes take place when at least five of the symptoms listed below are experienced almost daily for at least two weeks:

-Feelings of sadness, hopelessness, frustration, etc.

-Persistent and significant lack of energy

- Fatigue/tiredness regardless of physical activity or workload, particularly in the morning

- Significant anger, agitation, or irritability

- Changes in appetite and weight (loss or gain)

- Tendency to believe in negative ideas (e.g. "I'm worthless/useless", "It's my fault", etc.)

- Suicidal behaviour and ideation

Those who are depressed or experiencing depressive episodes also have a noticeably decreased capability to handle simple activities. Often, they experience being filled with anxiety, tearfulness, or irritability when tasked with minor conflicts or decisions.

In severe cases of depression, individuals may also experience bouts of psychosis (e.g. delusions or hallucinations).

In the same way, should you notice these symptoms, it's important that you call attention to them. Often, early detection is a great way to prevent a full-blown episode from happening since this allows your loved one to take the necessary medications and precautions that serve to stabilize them.

Though less severe, hypomania or hypomanic episodes are also emotional states you should watch out for.

Chapter 10: Lifestyle Changes And Home Remedies

Even though you are required to take medications to control the symptoms of your bipolar disorder that does not mean that you have to rely on it entirely for you to get better. There are plenty of things that you can do to naturally reduce the manic/depressive episodes brought about by your bipolar disorder, and it is recommended that you give them a try to give yourself more of a fighting chance against the monsters that are in your head.

Diet Changes

There is actually no such thing as a "bipolar diet", but there are certain kinds of foods that you need to avoid to reduce the instances and severity of your bipolar episodes. Generally, it is advisable for you to avoid Western-style diets that are chock-full of red meats, simple sugars and carbohydrates, and fats (saturated and trans). Avoiding these kinds of foods do not directly affect the symptoms associated with bipolar disorder, but they do somehow improve your mood.

It is also recommended that you avoid caffeine and simple sugars as they are quite potent stimulants. These substances will not only increase the severity of your manic episodes, they can also keep you up at night; and lack of sleep is said to make bipolar worse.

Exercise

Getting into the healthy habit of exercising regularly can greatly help in treating bipolar depression. Any kind of exercise can increase the natural production of endorphins and serotonin, these are basically the hormones responsible for controlling your moods. Endorphins block the pain receptors in your brain, and they also give you the general feeling of being happy. Serotonins on the other hand make you more relaxed; you will need to increase the production of this hormone if you are having problems sleeping.

Consult with your doctor to get advice on what kind of exercise regime would suit you best. Also remember to take it slow at first and only increase the intensity of your exercise program once your body has gotten used to the increase of physical activity.

Home Remedies and Supplements

With the rising costs of healthcare and medications, it is not really surprising that people are looking for low-cost, natural alternative remedies for everything that ails them, and patients diagnosed with bipolar disorder are no different. Alternative medicine looks at the mind and body as a whole, meaning one influences the other, which is why most of them focus on holistic care.

You can find alternative remedies and dietary supplements all over the internet and in most pharmacies, just remember to consult with your doctor before you use them to treat your bipolar disorder. Even though they are "natural" you should not assume that they do not carry any health risks or will not interfere with the efficacy of your prescription medication. There are some cases wherein the herbal supplements and prescription drugs did not have such a healthy interaction with each other; they sometimes even lead to more serious complications. Alternative medicines are not regulated by the FDA the same way they do prescription meds, so you should not really start self-medicating without consulting with your doctor first.

Always keep in mind that once you are diagnosed with bipolar disorder, from now on prescription medication will always be a part of your life. Even though there are "natural" means to boost your mood and help control your bipolar tendencies, they are not enough on their own, you will still need to take the medicines prescribed by your doctor if you want to live a somewhat normal life.

Chapter 11: Mania And Hypomania

As the name implies, Bipolar Disorder is about having extreme mood states. Mania and hypomania are the "up" states. The experience of having had either at some point in life defines the difference between Major Depression and Bipolar Depression. It is important to know what mania means.

Mania, the defining characteristic of Bipolar I Disorder

In mania, severe arousal changes last at least a week, and sometimes for many weeks. This extreme mood state can be one of euphoria, a top-of-the-world feeling, increased energy and activity, and constant restlessness and agitation. Sometimes this heightened arousal is experienced as a high degree of irritability all the way up to rage. Thoughts race through the mind and can't be slowed or stopped. A person is distractible, and thoughts and ideas seem to leap from one thing to another. When in a manic state, people are often unaware of how bad off they really are. Sometimes they report they enjoy being manic, and when they do strangely enjoy it, they resist treatment to normalize mood. Frequently, they miss the high in a manner not too dissimilar to missing the high of stimulant drugs like methamphetamine or cocaine. When in the manic state, a person experiences most of the following:

*Lack of need to sleep. Some report sleeping only 3 hours a night, while others amazingly get by with only cat naps.

*Poor judgment, irrational decision making, and indifference to the potential for adverse consequences of risky behavior. Overconfidence, inflated self-esteem, grandiose beliefs of being specially chosen and inordinately gifted. Some feel that they can fly, and then jump off a roof. Some bet the mortgage payment on the roulette wheel believing they are unable to lose. One person I knew had to be pulled off train tracks because he knew he couldn't be hurt by the oncoming train, saying like Superman, "I am faster than a speeding locomotive. I can stop that train with my mind."

*Hypersexual behavior, buying sprees with no thought of financial costs, driving too fast and recklessly. Speech is rapid fire, as if the racing thoughts must all expressed. Anyone trying to interrupt the non-stop talking is unable to break through. One unfortunate woman was so enchanted by a particular pair of shoes she saw on a television shopping network in the wee hours of a sleepless night that she then and there picked up the phone, called the television hosts, and bought several dozen pairs in every color available. She was quite the sensation to the television merchandisers. The box they came in was as big as the bill.
*Increased use of drugs and alcohol, particularly those that have a sedating

effect. Sometimes deep down somewhere they know they have to do something to slow down. Others want even more of a high, and pile on stimulant drugs that act like gasoline on a fire. In about half of manic episodes, people lose all touch with reality and need hospitalization. Like mentioned above, grandiose beliefs arise such as having extraordinary powers and being invincible to physical harm, or believing one is super wealthy and can spend without any care. Sometimes they will hear voices talking, laughing, or cursing with nobody actually there. They may come to believe there are malevolent forces seeking to do them harm, reading their thoughts or spying on them. Mistaking harmless remarks, gestures, or eye contact as signs of imminent attack, the manic person might strike out and seriously harm someone. Once a first manic episode has occurred, there is about a 90% chance of having more in the future if not treated. Untreated, the recurrence average is one episode every 1-3 years.

The preferred treatment is psychological therapy and support combined with mood stabilizing medication.

Hypomania, the defining characteristic of Bipolar II Disorder

As the name implies, hypomania is a milder form of mania, but the person is still operating at a much higher arousal level than his or her normal state.

Hypomania is often the trickiest to discern, because most people who experience this mood state find the increased energy, happy feelings, ability to work productively, clarity of thought, and increased sex drive to be pleasurable and positive. All of the signs and symptoms of mania can be present, but to a lesser degree and for a lesser amount of time.

Hypomania doesn't usually significantly disrupt social, work or school functioning.

Unrecognized and untreated hypomania can over time lead into full blown mania. Between 5-15% of hypomania patients go on to develop mania or a mixed manic and depressed episode.

Bipolar II Disorder is diagnosed slightly more frequently in women than in men.

Sometimes it's hard to tell objectively that a person is in a hypomanic arousal state or is just much more happy or irritable than usual. Those who never experience mania, but only the heightened arousal state of hypomania, often do not report such episodes to their doctors. Thus when they come in for their appointment in a deep depression, no one recognizes it to be Bipolar Depression and not Major Depression. As a consequence, standard antidepressant medications are usually given with advice to call back in a week or two to see how they are working.

Chapter 12: Protect Your Psychology

So far the equation is:

Natural products + Lifestyle = BPD overcome

Is this enough? Unfortunately no. You will need to address some more issues that will contribute to your psychology which is actually the most important factor of defeating any disease. These issues are:

1) Sleep.

One of the symptoms of bipolar disorder is sleep deprivation during the manic phase. But since the body needs to balance this, at the depression phase, it sleeps a lot. If BPD becomes a reason for the onset of anxiety this will become a sleeping nightmare.

Your body needs to receive enough rest at all times. If you can't sleep, use sedatives. If you can't wake up, use a rather loud alarm clock positioned away from your bed, so that you will have to get up to shut it down. What will the right amount of sleep do for you?

Make you less moody

Prevent you from feeling sick depressed or worried

Help you in decision making.

A few more things that you can do to get enough sleep are:

No drinking of alcohol or caffeine before going to bed.

Maintain the temperature of your bedroom at a constant comfortable level.

Keep your bedroom as dark as possible.

Do not exercise too late in the day.

Learn about relaxation techniques.

2) Do not avoid your medication

Some patients of bipolar disorder when they see that their symptoms are gone, stop taking their medication. This is a very big mistake. You should always keep taking your medication until the attending physician says otherwise. If you stop taking them too early the possibility of a relapse is too great. Keep taking them even if you detest the side effects. Keep in mind that most of them will be transient.

3) Include psychotherapy

Psychotherapy sessions, even interpersonal ones, are terribly important. Bipolar disorder is a psychic condition. It needs to be treated through access to the human psyche. It will help you greatly to correctly interpret what you see and what you perceive, and to understand what is going on in your mind.

4) Manage your condition at work

Work related issues are one of the most important factors for stress, anxiety BPD and all other mental conditions. Especially in a job that the boss applies more and more pressure for results, or, if you are the boss, you are pressuring yourself for results so that your business does well. Here is a list of what you can do during your working hours. If you are an employee a letter from your doctor will allow you to do them regardless of what your boss says:

Take regular breaks. If your stress levels rise, take a break before you think that you will explode in someone's face, or a depressing episode is knocking at your door.

Try deep breathing

Take a walk around the block and listen to relaxing music (not enough to make you asleep though!)

Call a friend or take some time off and visit your councilor.

5) DO NOT GIVE UP!

This is self-explanatory and its importance cannot be stressed enough. Repeatedly in this text it is mentioned that you need to want to get better. It's simple. Giving up means that you do NOT want to get better.

Now that these issues have been addressed, you are getting closer and closer to the desired and required result.

But there are still a few issues to take care off.

Chapter 13: Types Of Bipolar Therapy

As mentioned earlier, medications are not enough. So, if you want your therapy to be successful, you must go to therapy. There are many types of therapies that are available for bipolar disorder, including:

1. Psychotherapy

Psychotherapy is also called talk therapy. This type of therapy will help you sort out your issues. Your psychotherapist can also give you helpful tips on how to deal with the symptoms of bipolar disorder and how to manage your moods.

Cognitive Behavior Therapy

This type of psychotherapy focuses on behaviors that help decrease stress. Your psychotherapist may give you tips and techniques on how to control your emotions and moods. Your therapist may also give techniques on how to effectively respond to stressful and difficult situations.

Interpersonal Therapy

This type of therapy requires the participation of the people you love. It helps examine relationships. It helps identify the relationship problems that may be caused by the illness.

Social Rhythm Therapy

People with bipolar disorder has to establish routines in their life. This strategy helps control mood swings and cycling. Social rhythm therapy helps you develop normal sleep schedules and routines.

2. Light and Dark Therapy

This type of therapy focuses on the sensitive circadian rhythm of people with mental health issues. The goal of this therapy is to manipulate our circadian rhythms that heavily affect the function of neurotransmitters and hormones. During manic episodes, dark therapy will help control insomnia. Light therapy may also help alleviate the moods of people with bipolar disorder during depressive episodes.

3. Acupuncture

Acupuncture is a great supplemental treatment for people with bipolar disorder. This treatment was developed in China and has been used to treat various medical conditions for over two thousand years. Acupuncture can help bipolar patients regulate their response to stress and difficult situations. Acupuncture treatment also stimulates the production of certain brain chemicals like endorphins, dopamine, and serotonin. To reap the full benefits of acupuncture, you must see your acupuncturist at least once a week.

4. Mindfulness Meditation

Studies show that mindfulness meditation can help reduce the symptoms of bipolar disorder by keeping the patient grounded with the reality.

Here's how you can use mindfulness to manage the symptoms of bipolar disorder:

Sit on a chair and then close your eyes.

Start to take deep breaths.

As you inhale, say quietly "inhaling". As you exhale, say "exhaling".

If distracting thoughts enter your mind, you have to gently redirect your thoughts back to your breath.

Say a silent prayer of gratitude. Then open your eyes.

To reap the full benefits of mindfulness meditation, you have to do this every day for at least a month. You can meditate for 3 to 5 minutes during your first week and then you can increase your meditation time as you progress.

Here's another technique that you can use to manage your symptoms:

Sit on a chair and take deep breaths.

Watch how your chest go up and down as you breathe.

Then, focus your attention on your head. Notice sensations in your head. Do you feel pain? Is your head itchy?

Then, move your attention to your neck, chest, shoulders, arms, fingers, belly, pelvis, buttocks, legs, and feet.

Pay attention to the sensations that you feel in each part of your body.

If distracting thoughts enter your mind, try to focus your attention back to your body.

It's good to play a relaxing music during your meditation session. It's also best to set an alarm or a timer. This way, you will not be disturbed.

5. Music Therapy

Music therapy is a potent treatment for various mental health disorders, including bipolar disorder. It helps calm your mind during mania and lift up your spirit during depression. Music is a deep emotional experience so in a sense, it can improve the symptoms of bipolar disorder.

Music heals your heart. It increases relaxation and it reduces loneliness. It also provides emotional release and it establishes a strong spiritual connection. You can use music therapy along with medication and lifestyle change.

6. Massage Therapy

Massage helps manage the symptoms of bipolar disorder as it helps reduce stress and anxiety. It also helps balance the levels of neurotransmitters such as serotonin, dopamine, epinephrine, and norepinephrine.

If you have a bipolar disorder, it is essential to subject yourself to therapy. Therapy can help sort out your issues. It can also help you develop that can help you manage your bipolar disorder.

Chapter 14: Learn How To Deal With The Things That Will Stress Your Mind Out

It has been found that the most stressful and demanding events that occur in our everyday lives can play a critical role in how the symptoms of this disorder affects you. It has also been found that the way you can avoid an episode or attack is possible to achieve if you only learn how to control your everyday stress levels.

People with bipolar disorder are normal people, just like anybody else and they go through the same problem as everybody else: worrying about their family, worrying about their health and stressing over their financial future. The best way to manage and control your stress levels is to use your God given skills to help deal with the problems that arise in your life on a daily basis.

In this chapter you will learn different methods that you can use to help manage your stress and to have fewer depressive and manic attacks every single day.

The Best Way To Cope With Your Stressors

Step One: Identify Your Stressors-You will only be able to identify and define your problems if you are aware of the fact that problems do exist and they will inevitably come into your life. There are a variety of both internal and external signals that can be useful in identifying a problem as it occurs.

Your internal signals can include changes in your physical body like tension in your muscles, constant headache, changes in how you breathe and tension in your chest. These changes in your physical body can work as signals of stress that can prompt you that you have unsolved problems that require your attention. You can also observe changes in your emotions such as feeling hopeless and being anxious and worried. These changes in your emotions can also prompt you that you have existing unsolved problems.

Step Two: Prioritize Your Issues-It is quite common for people suffering from bipolar disorder to go through major problems after a dramatic manic or depressive episode. For instance, you may be faced with financial issues when you become unemployed as a result of your constant fatigue and low enthusiasm during a depressive episode.

Similarly, a manic episode can make you go through expensive shopping sprees that can also result to financial issues that you will have to deal with after the manic episode has passed. You may feel frustrated, hopeless and overwhelmed when you realize the gravity of your problems and you might be tempted to think that it doesn't seem possible to solve your problems especially when you cannot think of the right place to start.

Step Three: Determine What Your Coping Resources Are-Your coping resources are basically internal and external assets that you can call upon to help you to conquer the priority problems that you have identify. Your external assets or resources include support from other people who understand your predicament such as your loved ones, your doctor and your colleagues from work.

You can also get support from people who are not directly connected to you such as support agencies and your own financial assets. Your internal assets or resources include your own intelligence, creativity, determination, ingenuity, sense of humor and compassion, among other.

Step Four: Determine What Problems Can Block Your Coping Resources-Whether you like it or not, you will also encounter stumbling blocks that will hinder you from effectively coping with your problems. These stumbling blocks can also be both internal (such as limiting beliefs, impaired judgment and fearfulness) and external (such as tight deadlines, inadequate resources, and lack of information). You need to determine your own stumbling blocks so you can minimize them as you try to solve your problems.

Step Five: Overcome The Obstacles That Block Your Coping Resources-After you have determined your own stumbling blocks, it is quite essential that you face them and think of ways on how you can conquer them so you can better cope with your problems. There may be times when you may have to challenge your own beliefs to get past your stumbling blocks. Always keep in mind that it is ok to seek assistance or advice from other people.

Chapter 15: Techniques To Lower Your Stress

Stress has been linked to many health issues and mental health can be especially at risk. Bipolar sufferers react to stress much more strongly than others which is why it is often the catalyst for swings. Avoiding stress altogether is preferable but with our busy daily lives it's close to impossible to manage. There are many stress reduction techniques out there that you can use every day. These include breathing exercises, meditation, and yoga. But other than the obvious there are specific actions you can do to de-stress yourself after the fact so your overall stress level lowers.

Try Hobbies

Hobbies are a great way to relax and can also help keep your mind from wandering to overblown or stressful thoughts. Many hobbies can also be forms of exercise which are doubly useful for those with bipolar. Activities like swimming, gardening, hiking, and cycling are all fairly strenuous and can be part of an active lifestyle as well as soothing hobbies. Hobbies can also help improve focus by forcing you to concentrate on a specified action for a length of time. Dancing has also been shown to have its own unique mood lifting properties and is an excellent cardiovascular workout.

For those looking for a less strenuous hobby, painting, drawing, and writing are all ideal ways of purging negative thoughts. Many famous artists had tortured minds and used their art or writing to get thoughts and feelings out and stop them from affecting their daily lives. Creative hobbies are common among sufferers and many groups also offer a social setting to meet like-minded individuals. This can help combat the isolationism of depression.

Other hobby activities can also be social but can be spiritually uplifting too. Volunteering or joining outreach programs is an ideal way to feel needed and to help foster self-esteem. By helping others less fortunate you can combat those thoughts of worthlessness created by the disease. This is a way of sharing that also helps to give a feeling of accomplishment and boosting mood.

Pets/Therapy Animals

Many people have pets but they don't always realize how important they can be. Most animals have a strong, unconditional love for their owners or can be trained to react to certain symptoms. Therapy animals are often more aware of our own symptoms than we are and can react to emotional or chemical changes with training and help owners stop a spiral. Training therapy animals is quite hard but they can be the only way of getting the emotional support you need 24 hours a day. For some people, an emotional support animal can be the only way they can function in a stressful environment.

To qualify for a trained support animal you must have an official diagnosis, but you can also register existing pets and have them trained. Therapy animals come in all shapes and sizes, there's even someone with a turkey bird! Having an animal that loves you can help life your mood significantly and for some taking care of a pet can give meaning to their daily life since the animal relies on them too.

Example Tim:

Tim has a support dog, they go everywhere together. While in a supermarket one day he gets yelled at by another customer over a parking space. During the disagreement, Tim's stress level rises. The dog is trained to react, it begins to lick him and tries to focus his attention away from the irate customer. The customer eventually leaves Tim alone but he is feeling very drained after the encounter and starts to think depressive thoughts. His dog continues to shower him with love forcing Tim's focus to the animal. As he pets the dog Tim calms down and his mood improves.

Treatment

Stressful situations should be avoided if possible but it's close to impossible with modern life. Start by using anti-stress techniques if you're feeling triggered and consider getting a therapy animal to help you. Hobbies are also a great way to de-stress as they provide pleasure, joy, and can give you social interaction which counters depressive isolationism.

Chapter 16: Taking Accountability

Learning to take accountability for your actions is part of growing up. Many people find excuses to explain certain behaviors or personality traits and do nothing to change them. When a person has bipolar, it may seem that every mood swing or behavior they exhibit is because of bipolar. They may say that they can't help but act a certain way because they are bipolar. They are not taking accountability for their actions when everything they do or say is "because of bipolar." When there is another spouse involved, and disagreements inevitably ensue, it is important for both people to take accountability. This can help resolve the disagreements and provide insight into avoiding them in the future, or at least avoiding the same severity of disagreements. When both people take accountability for themselves, and do not blame the other person, it shows that both people are willing to grow and change from the experience.

Bipolar or not, everybody is responsible for their actions. Having bipolar is not a blanket excuse for all erratic behavior. Even with a mood disorder, a bipolar person still has an abundance of choices to make every day. Bipolar does help explain the source of erratic behavior, however. Even though you may feel like acting deplorably, you may have a choice to step away for the moment, before acting on an impulse.

I realize that even though I have bipolar, and I may be prone to certain behaviors, I still have a responsibility to do what I can to minimize those symptoms so that the people around me don't have to experience severe mood swings with me. Now, there's not a lot I can do to change the illness, but I can try and assess my moods throughout the day. If there is a period of time where I'm struggling, I can make changes to the environment to help reduce the severity of my mood change. And, if I happen to yell at someone or lose my cool, I have to admit to myself that I let my illness get the better of me. I didn't do what was necessary to avoid that behavior, so I have to be accountable for my actions. If I learn from those situations now, I won't repeat the same behavior at a later time. This can go a long way with your spouse as well since they can see you are willing to admit when you need to change.

When disagreements occur within the relationship, both people must take accountability for their own actions. Most disagreements or fights have two sides to the story, and there are ways for both people to change. The opposite of taking accountability would be blaming the other person for their behavior without acknowledging your own behavior. A bipolar person may blame their spouse for not understanding what they go through on a daily basis rather than admit that their behavior was unacceptable. They may also blame the illness for the behavior taking place to begin with. On the flip side, the spouse without bipolar may blame the other person for having the illness and acting crazy. None of these scenarios will help the couple move forward and grow from the experience. Communicating with one another about what went wrong and how both people can avoid blaming each other in the future is a healthier way to approach a solution. My spouse and I used to get into disagreements over my behavior, but instead of blaming the illness, he wouldn't even acknowledge that I had an illness. He still maintains to this day that my problems are ordinary problems that occur with every person, and that I don't act like I have bipolar. I finally gave up trying to convince him, because my well-being is not dependent on whether he believes I have bipolar or not. This actually makes it easier for me NOT to use bipolar as an excuse for my behavior, since he won't even accept that as an answer. Now we just try to communicate what is bothering us about the other person without blaming each other. We try to admit our own faults as much as possible. We get to the root of the problem much quicker and resolve the conflict in a much healthier way.

Chapter 17: Chronotherapy, Sleep Deprivation And Melatonin

Chronotherapy, one of the more peculiar methods in this guide, is a practice that refers to the shifting of your sleep schedule. It may seem odd to alter or shift your sleep schedule, especially when trying to deal with a mental disorder. However, while this is generally true, it has many benefits when it comes to helping those suffering from symptoms of bipolar disorder. The main one of these benefits, as with so many treatments, is acting as a proficient mood stabilizer. Here, we will look at how the shifting of sleep schedules, in addition to other factors of chronotherapy, can help regulate mood, and how that regulation of mood creates a better life overall.

When shifting your sleep time in accordance with chronotherapy, there are several ways to do it. You could sleep either earlier or later, less or more. Each shift will be different based on the person, but this form of therapy simply connotes a change to your normal sleeping habits. By shifting these habits, you set a rigid schedule that will help you conform to the new way of sleeping. Creating this new schedule will help in two different ways. One, it has been found to create a strict control of the sleep-wake cycle. Two, it also has been shown to create a certain control over the light-dark rhythms. Each of these have shown to allow for better moods in bipolar patients, and they have also been shown to have mood stabilizing effects. However, this will only be effective when control over the sleep schedule is achieved. Putting yourself into a tight, rigid schedule will give you the necessary control that you need.

When trying to implement a certain type of sleep schedule, it may be beneficial to take medication that will help you fall asleep. There are many options for this, but melatonin is one of the most effective. Melatonin, chemically known as N-acetyl-5-methoxytryptamine, is a naturally occurring hormone that helps regulate the light-dark cycle in living organisms. This is why it can be such an effective sleep aid. When you are trying to create a new sleep cycle, aids such as melatonin can be very effective at helping you fall sleep at a certain time. If you do take melatonin, which is ingested orally through either capsules, tablets, or liquid, it is best to take it 3-6 milligrams. This can also be useful for people suffering from melatonin deficiency as well. This medication is best taken around 9 pm.

Another important element chronotheraputic treatment is sleep deprivation. Just as with the shifting of your sleeping schedule, actively taking part is sleep deprivation can have some less-than-desired results. However, these effects, which will be covered later, can be worth it if chronotherapy or sleep deprivation is found to help your mental health. Sleep deprivation is a process that has been seen to help those suffering from depression. Depression caused from bipolar disorder can have some negative effects, and though it might seem strange, choosing to not sleep can reverse some of these negativities.

When using sleep deprivation, it is best to start slow before taking shorter and shorter periods of sleep. There are two types of sleep deprivation, and both can be effective at battling depression. The first of these is partial sleep deprivation. Here, the patient doesn't avoid sleep, but rather just only sleeps for short periods every night. These periods usually last around 3 to 4 hours, and acts as a way to still get some rest while losing sleep. The other, and more extreme, method of sleep deprivation is total sleep deprivation. In this method, the patient simply avoids sleep for long periods of time. Here, sleep avoidance can last days, going as long as 40 hours.

While not sleeping for 40 hours can put strains on your body, to minimize the risks of sleep deprivation, each awake period is followed by what is called a recovery sleep. That is a longer period of sleep, which gives your body a chance to rest. The results of sleep deprivation in this manner have been recorded through numerous trials as well as small studies (Ravindran et al., Journal of Affective Disorders. 2013; 150:707). Researchers have found that sleep deprivation has mullti-modal influences on mood, involving impact on thyroid hormone levels. In addition, it has also been found to have effects on metabolic and monoaminergic functioning as well. All of these benefits, in addition to curbing depression, were noted more in people suffering from bipolar disorder who underwent the treatment than those not suffering from the disorder.

As taking part in sleep deprivation can cause added stress or fatigue to your body, there are some side effects from using this method. Most are minimal, but all focus on the toll the treatment can have. These effects are headache, fatigue, gastrointestinal symptoms, sleepiness, and worsening of depression or hypomania in vulnerable patients. Some of these may be uncomfortable, but, as previously stated, it is always a good idea to use treatments that work best for you. Every method is going to have some ramifications, but if you can manage to find one that helps your symptoms, then that is the one you should use.

Chapter 18: What Is The Worst Part Of Having Borderline Personality Disorder?

Most of the time it really doesn't cause me problems, on a day to day basis. So I suppose the worst part would be when I find someone I like enough to idealize. That sort of brings it all out of me for some reason.

I become dependent on the person when normally I don't interact with other people on more than a superficial level. Suddenly, this person is the whole universe. Everything is them and they are everything. Which generally makes people uncomfortable. Especially when it's such a drastic change from my normal self. I'm pretty much a completely different person like that. And not one that's sought after either.

At that point it's like the secret hidden two year old inside me comes out and makes itself very, very obvious. Where before I wouldn't talk to the person all day, then show up six hours after I'd said I'd be there, now I want to be around them all the time. Like a toddler, I need constant attention.

Then I start hating myself because I don't like that two year old and I don't want to remember she exists. I certainly don't want anyone else to see her. She's weak and pathetic. I hate thinking about it now even just to write about it.

Usually the other person starts hating me too. Or maybe that's in my head, I don't know. Regardless I behave as though they can't stand the two year old because I certainly can't. How could someone else? Maybe I ruin it at that point or maybe they do, I'm still not sure which it is. But the other person leaves. I think it freaks them out.

That's when the devaluing starts. They saw the horrible two year old and didn't like it so they left. I don't like it either but I can't leave it or keep it hidden. That pisses me off. I hate myself for having her in me, for letting people see her, and I hate them even more for being afraid of it and leaving me to figure out how to lock her back up by myself.

And then I try to kill myself. Every time. I guess maybe I'm trying to get rid of the two year old even if I have to throw the rest out with it.

I try not to idealize people anymore. Luckily it rarely happens anyway. It always ends badly. That's definitely the absolute worst part of BPD for me.

What is it like being friends with someone with borderline personality disorder?

My opinion doesn't necessarily fit the same mold as other BPD's or BPD(NOS), honestly, even AvBPD...we all have different personality traits and behavioral differences.

But...in general, it isn't fun. It's an emotional rollercoaster on NOS that has turns at g forces that would rip your face off. Lows so low that they would send you to the bowels of Mordor for a five week vacay. Meals, bar and tips included.

For me and my friends, it is a constant...hey...are you still alive? How come you aren't on Facebook anymore? Did you block me? And a constant revolving door of friends....with only a small hand of close ones that stick with me.

It's not easy. Sometimes it's *GREAT!* Sometimes it's lonely. I have my three or four who text me every couple of months to make sure I am still breathing. We will send a snapchat or two. Maybe a text. I will abruptly stop and that will be that for a few more months. And the cycle starts again. I never call on the phone. I hate phone calls. But it's touch and go. Never steady. You can't rely on me. Not when I am in a "phase". When I am not in a "phase"...I am fun and funny! Come over for drinks...lets go to the club! But I might get jealous..and then I'll panic...and uh oh! It's a shit show!

But I do have lucid times when I am normal, and I control my behaviors for the most part. And I can interact socially quite well and normally. Most wouldn't even know that I am "damaged goods". I go to car shows with my 2010 Camaro 2SS, chat it up with other car enthusiasts, help a grease monkey tighten a clamp or two.

I'll host game night of Cards Against Humanity with my husband's coworkers and their wives at my home, and make sure everyone is fed well, served drinks, has a great time and wants to come back the next weekend! I make baby blankets for any expecting ladies at the local Sheriff's Department where my husband works.

But during a bad phase, I am constantly deleting social media. Because I think someone is mad at me, or slighting me, when most likely they are not. It's the classic "making a mountain of a molehill". But I will see it no other way and convince myself of it. Sometimes so much so I will unfriend someone or even block them. They won't even know what happened. I have lost so many friends that way. I have lost family members this way as well.

It is a lonely existence sometimes because it is always revolving...it comes and goes in cycles. But most normal people can't stand the ups and downs that it brings. The ups and downs that I bring. And I only do it to myself.

Is it possible for a person with borderline personality disorder to change?

Yes.

It's kinda impossible to change away from the stigma surrounding the disorder, though, because the stigma pertains to things that don't exist.

So really the answer depends upon what you mean by 'BPD', but BPD as understood by Marsha Linehan is something that can certainly evolve into something like

'BPD+'; self-compassion can bring about remarkable change in someone who hasn't known what this is before, and with *the right self-compassion for BPD...*

...I couldn't have imagined the way I feel today as little as 2–3yrs ago. I don't want to spoil it but there are hidden talents within our empathy paradigm... that... I mean...

Yeah. Facilitation, yo! DBT didn't do it all for me, but it set me on the right path with the right principles and I have no problem with rocking those as hard as possible forever.

Not a day goes by when I'm not grateful for my life now I can put said life into a bit of context. Results vary, of course — and also DBT isn't available everywhere and to everyone, but in principle anyone can change. I mean... *we do change,* in affect, probably relatively frequently compared to neurotypical folks, and that's a big part of dysregulation...

...but I'm guessing you're talking remediation rather than symptomicity here.

Change can be *a little* messy at times, and change of the kind implied by therapy is necessarily an intimidating prospect because it pertains to the brain, interpersonal relationships and that most nebulous of concepts 'personality'...

...but if we change relatively frequently anyhow ...I mean ...I dunno. It's all good!

Hope this helps! :)

Do all people with borderline personality disorder discard their lovers?

I have BPD, and I know that one of the symptoms of BPD is discarding people after an idealization phase when the devaluation phase occurs.

It's hard for people with BPD to hold a person as a whole in their head at all times; if a person does something to them that triggers them they will often forget all the good things they knew about a person and see them as all bad.

When a person with BPD is triggered by perceived abandonment, rejection, criticism, etc. they usually want to act out on that pain, because that pain to them is something they do not want to feel at any cost, but they don't know the rational way to act out on it i.e. discussing things or finding a beneficial mutual solution, i.e. cooperation. They only have their own defense mechanisms available (or, what's more likely, they may have other options available to them, but it's too difficult to STOP the process that occurs and has occurred for so long - the process of being triggered by something, feeling all the emotions that go along with that, acting out on those emotions in order to reduce or stop them, and then the resulting fallout from acting out) which are crude and blunt and unfortunately might mean discarding you in order to prevent you from causing them more pain.

Once the discard has occurred, if a person with BPD is at a point where they can realize that they might have acted rashly, it might be too painful for them to bear the guilt/shame in what they've done, so they might convince themself that they really do hate you because it's easier than feeling the shame at having acted so outrageously.

Or they might in fact realize it and feel immense regret... They might be too ashamed to apologise and try to correct things, so again they might convince themself that they truly do hate you in order to not have to feel regret and not have to apologise. (They sure do hate themselves though. Believe that. Often we walk around feeling like the scum of the earth). It's not really the apology that they want to avoid, it's the shame that accompanies it.

Or maybe even they dissociate and feel nothing after an outburst or altercation or whatever you want to call it, after a discard. They don't want to feel regret, or shame or anything, so they just go completely blank.

Often the initial thing that triggered the person with BPD can be something that has been misconstrued by the person with

BPD as an act of rejection or abandonment or an attack of some sort or some other negative thing, even if you are a good person who has been kind and acted relatively normally during the duration of the relationship, and this person knows this about you, and you imagine that they trust you. But it can still happen, this misconstruction of motives. It's because there's a lot of baggage that someone with BPD carries around in order to 'stop the pain' - a lot of templates that have been stored in their brain, like short-circuits that exist to protect them. If person A does thing B and says thing C then it must mean D and they must be stopped/discarded/ignored/hurt by revenge/etc. They fail to come up with realistic alternatives, fail at reality testing (maybe that's the term for it, I'm not sure).

What advice would you give someone who was recently diagnosed with BPD, borderline personality disorder?

Don't dwell too much on your diagnosis

Definitely do not google BPD or go down the rabbit hole of discussion boards on BPD

Resist the urge to overshare you diagnosis with others (outside of immediate loved ones) I understand the concept of becoming an "anti-stigma martyr" but in reality you will just be shooting yourself in the foot.

DO NOT tell your boss or co-workers about your diagnosis. This will not foster greater understanding. We would like to think that the world is progressive enough to understand mental health, but we still have a long way to go.

I actually had a co-worker (someone I thought was quite open minded) say to me (unprovoked referring to a difficult client) that she could just tell when someone was "cluster B" because "they made the hair on the back of her neck stand up" like evil has just entered the room.

I wanted so badly to ask her how she felt talking to *me* right now. But I resisted the urge. As much as I would love to school every person I meet about their ignorance surrounding mental health, I have to live my life too. Maybe one day.

Learn about your disorder

Learn about your disorder only from legitimate scholarly resources.

Know thyself, becoming good at observing yourself objectively can help you pull yourself out of an emotional state.

knowing what being triggered feels like and managing that feeling rather than reacting etc.

Join a DBT group

There can be long wait lists, but the wait is definitely worth it.

Once in DBT, give it a real chance

When I first started DBT I hated it, which is probably a good sign that it might work. Change is never comfortable, and so many of the concepts just sounded so touchy feely, or stupid, or just plain wrong (what do you mean I am *choosing* to act on my emotions!?) but there's a reason why a DBT programme is generally repeated three times, it really took me that long to finally have it click.

Practice self-compassion, recovery is legitimately hard.

Take a non-mentally ill person and try to teach them how to see the world totally differently, have them relearn values, change their perception and basically relearn everything that they have ever learned about the world up to this point in time. You are essentially having your core reparented, only now you are an adult with preconceptions and a history, your brain is less plastic and you are set in your ways. BPD is a ***personality*** disorder, this means that recovery involves changing certain parts of your personality. No easy feat for anyone. But it is possible.

There is a reason that you are the way that you are

BPD does not exist in a vacuum. For people suffering from BPD who have not suffered clear cut recognizable "abuse" this fact in and of itself is invalidating. Someone who was born with a different more sensitive more intense temperament from care givers or the rest of their family may have a fairly normal upbringing, but constantly having their hyper sensitive feelings and perceptions invalidated by those around them can cause a never ending cycle of invalidation

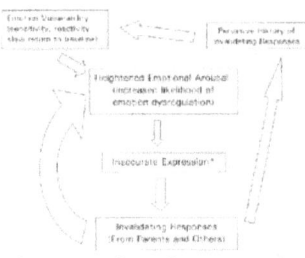

The Idea that only those who have been sexually abused develop BPD is false, it is actually the ignoring of the abuse by others or the failure of caregivers to recognize and stop the abuse that causes the extreme invalidation of the individuals suffering from the abuse. The subsequent

development of maladaptive coping mechanisms in order to deal with the feelings of invalidation are the cause of BPD. This feeling of not being seen, the feelings of suffering alone as a child can happen for a variety of reasons and is not at all mutually exclusive to physical and sexual abuse.

In recovery, at some point you *will* become very angry with care givers

This is the part where you learn about Radical Acceptance This for most people is the hardest part of DBT and recovery. I myself still struggle with this.

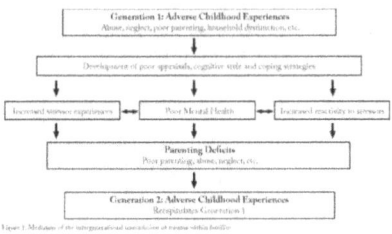

Figure 1. Mediators of the intergenerational transmission of trauma within families

I try to remember that my parents weren't born in a vacuum either, my grandparents where abusive and (to my parent's benefit) far worse than my parents are. But I'm still angry. I still have a hard time reminding myself that they can't help the way that they are. I can no longer see my parents the way that I used too. I no longer see them as having power over me, but I also no longer idolize them either. They are just people now. People that a lot of the time I don't really like very much or have much in common with. In letting go of the hope that one day they will be the people who I need them to be, I have regained some of myself. But I still feel resentment. I hope one day to be able to let it go. but its hard (and that's OK too)

Above all, try to remember that we are all just doing the best that we can with what tools we have, and you have the power to build a new utility belt and become F*#$ing batman if you want to.

Putting on my DBT skills in the morning

Chapter 19: Exercise And Light Therapy

Exercise can help improve your child's bipolar disorder. Exercise causes the brain to release endorphins. Endorphins are known as feel-good hormones. Feel good hormones increase moods and they also relieve stress, which is one of the triggers of this disorder. However, for some exercising can become an obsession and over-exercising can trigger bipolar mania.

You need to incorporate three elements of fitness in your child's exercise routine – endurance, strength, and flexibility.

Regular aerobic activity helps kids develop endurance. Aerobic activity strengthens the heart and improves the body's ability to deliver oxygen to all body cells. Aerobic activities include:

Running

Jogging

Walking

Tennis

Swimming

Soccer

Inline skating

Ice skating

Bicycling

Basketball

Instead of lifting weights, your kid can do pull-ups, push-ups, stomach crunches and other exercises to help tone and strengthen muscles. They can also improve their strength when they do a handstand, climb or wrestle.

Stretching exercises also help improve flexibility. Stretching allows muscles and joints to bend and offers a full range of motion. Kids stretch when they practice a split, do a cartwheel or reach for a toy.

Keep exercise activity fun, so your kid stays interested.

The sedentary problem

Kids now spend a few hours every day in front of a screen (TVs, tablets, smartphones, and other devices). Too much screen time and not enough physical activity can lead to a variety of physical and mental problems.

The American Academy of Pediatrics recommends parents:

Limits the time kids spend watching TV, playing video games or on social media.

Limit screen time to 1 hour daily.

Keep computers, TVs, and video games out of children's bedrooms and turn off screens during mealtimes.

Light Therapy Boxes

As a complement to psychotherapy, medication, and a lifestyle wellness plan, light therapy boxes may be a viable option. The box provides a balanced spectrum light equivalent to natural daylight. This therapy can help regulate the biological clock function and help synchronize sleep/wake patterns by providing a balanced spectrum light equivalent to natural daylight. Remember, using the lightbox for too long or too fast exposure can trigger a manic symptom of bipolar disorder. So, careful about the timing of using this box.

Lastly, the RAINBOW approach helps bipolar children reach their goal by promoting stability both internally and externally. With the RAINBOW approach, your family and child's treatment team help the child stay in the middle of the mood spectrum as much as possible using these strategies:

R: Routine to encourage a stable schedule

A: Affect (mood) regulation and Anger control

I: "I can do it"—positive self-talk to build self-esteem

N: No Negative thoughts

B: Be a good friend (for your child) and lead a balanced lifestyle

(For you)

O: Optimal problem solving

W: Ways to get support—for the child and the rest of your family

Chapter 20: Maintaining A Healthy Lifestyle

Many people with manic depression effect some lifestyle changes to help them stay healthy. These changes may be quite small ones such as remembering to use medication and mindfulness about sleep; however, some make considerable changes like changing jobs or adopting a quieter lifestyle in a rural area. It is known that the lifestyle of people with the disorder may affect their stress levels, and help minimize triggers and symptoms. You can make lifestyle choices that can help you live a fulfilling life regardless of your bipolar disorder but it's not advisable to make any major lifestyle decisions such as leaving a job or ending a relationship when the illness is at its peak, as you may not be rational in those moments. What you can do instead is to take time out to get healthy and stay healthy and then decide on things. This chapter explores ways of staying healthy and enriching life. We'll also talk about various good habits including exercise, healthy diet, stress management, and avoiding toxic substances.

Living well involves striking a balance between monitoring your illness and focusing on living your life in a manner that does not damage your health and allows you to enjoy life. Some people have ongoing symptoms in between episodes of bipolar disorder. Depressive symptoms are often the most persistent and disruptive.

You don't need to be constantly preoccupied with the illness when you are well, but regularly using your medications, keeping regular appointments with your doctor, and monitoring your triggers, mood and warning symptoms will help you take care of your illness while getting on with daily life. You can implement your relapse prevention plans at this time if necessary.

Sleep and mood go hand in hand. Sleep deprivation or disruption can very easily trigger mood episodes; hence part of your healthy lifestyle routine might include a general daily activity structure that is just stimulating enough and helps you to keep up regular activity levels throughout the day so you can maintain regular sleep habits. Some normal things like work stress, jet lag, and shift work might disrupt your sleep and you might need to make difficult decisions about them. If your routine or sleep has been cut short or interrupted, you may feel a bit up or excited, but instead of taking that as go-ahead to run around doing all sorts of things, take things easy and restore your usual sleep and routine patterns. There are many ways to enrich your daily life, such as engaging in meaningful activities.

Relationships

Relationships are not always enjoyable, but when they are, they can be rewarding and help promote your wellness. There are ways you can handle interpersonal problems and maintain good relationships.

Your family and friends, colleagues, and everyone you meet in your various areas of interests all serve as an opportunity for social interaction. Some people prefer using Internet chat-rooms specifically for people with bipolar disorder or attending meetings with their local support group because they often feel accepted and valued by these groups. They also report that apart from receiving help when needed, they find joy in helping others and being able to share their knowledge and experience with others.

They are also able to caution people and teach them that not all strategies for managing bipolar disorder work for everyone. Note that this advice may be subjective to their state of mind. Personal experience is priceless, but sometimes what people need is medical advice. With these cautions in mind, clearly other people living with bipolar disorder and their families are a great resource, and these networks can also create good friendships. They can provide essential services such as housing, employment, support, drop-in services, activity programs and advocacy.

Participating In Life

Life often involves various activities, including ones that relieve stress or give pleasure, and those that you derive a deep sense of satisfaction from because they enable you to use your talents or agree with your value system. However, a one-sided focus on achievement alone can cause you to set unrealistic goals for yourself as well as drive you to chase your goals in a way that will harm your health. Alternatively, relaxing and doing very little can make you feel purposeless and lethargic. Therefore, it is beneficial to pursue realistic and meaningful goals in a way that enhances your feeling of satisfaction without posing a danger to your health. Continuously chasing a goal can trigger a spin into mania and hypomania; people often find it beneficial to take regular break to relax. After engaging in stimulating activities, give yourself time to relax and unwind to help you stay on track.

It can be helpful to view your goals as journeys instead of a single entity, as this will help you understand that achieving the final goal is not the focal point, but that the small steps in the process of achieving the goal are the elements that enrich your life. Your self-esteem can be destroyed by setting unrealistic goals and disruptive episodes of illness. Setting realistic goals and achieving them can enhance your self-esteem and sense of fulfillment.

Setting SMART goals

The acronym SMART can aid realistic goal setting. Ensure that your goal is Specific, Measurable, Achievable, Realistic, and Timely.

Specific - You must have a specific goal so that you know when you have achieved it. For instance, saying, "I want to get fitter" is not a specific enough goal. Instead, you could say, "I'm planning to go swimming three times a week."

Measurable - Having a measurable goal helps you to plan the things you want to do and also to know when you have achieved such goal. E.g., "I plan to go swimming three times a week" could be put in even more measurable terms, such as "I'm planning to swim twenty laps of the local pool three times weekly."

Achievable - When setting a goal, ensure that it is a goal that can be achieved. You may be required to check for the barriers that may hinder your goal; for instance, your plan to swim twenty laps three times weekly may be possible if you have not exercised in actual time. Try to set a lower goal of five laps when you start. Also, divide big or long-term goals into smaller, more achievable steps. By doing this, the longer-term goal doesn't seem so huge. Coupled with this, you'll derive a sense of satisfaction from achieving the steps along the way. You may need to make a distinction between short-term goals with a timeframe of a day to one week or two, medium-term goals that can be achieved in a few weeks or months, and long-term goals that will require months or even years to achieve. Achieving your short-term goals remind you of your capabilities while longer-term goals that are meaningful to you can give you a sense of satisfaction and purpose in life.

Realistic - Setting a realistic goal helps you question your own practicality, and this can be a hard one. We all have limitations on our abilities and what goals are viable.

To set a realistic goal, you should consider and weigh the:

Conclusion

As you have seen in this book, we have prescribed different steps for how you can live a productive life with bipolar disorder. If you think of how many artists, musicians, and actors have lived with the disorder, you can see that anyone can be successful even with a bipolar disorder diagnosis. Carrie Fisher, whom we have quoted above, is an example of a successful actress, who has been able to live with bipolar disorder throughout her life. It hasn't been easy. Coping has been a difficult part of the process, but she has done well and has been able to survive and thrive with the disorder. If she can do it, so can you.

In this book, we have been able to look at the following things:

1. Understand the symptoms, diagnosis, and causes of bipolar disorder.

2. Discuss treatment options including medication, psychotherapy, CBT, and social therapy.

3. Discuss the various kinds of medications that you can take.

4. Talk about having suicidal thoughts and what you can do about it.

5. Explain what steps you can take to improve your wellness routine.

We hope that we have been able to more than adequately address these topics in this book, which is rather concise but packed with helpful information. We would like you to consider each topic from this book and apply the steps that you can to your life. You can live a meaningful life with bipolar disorder and thrive in your life.

Let's return to the example of Timothy. He is a fictional character based on a real-life story.

Timothy was able to get his bipolar disorder under control. He was able to seek the treatment that he needed in order to live a good life. He was able to travel to New Zealand and do an internship with a working holiday visa. He finally got his dream come true and got to meet a lot of friends there. Eventually, he decided to enroll in a Ph.D. program in ecology from the University of California Santa Barbara. After one year, he had a relapse and had to seek treatment for his anxiety and worry. It was wreaking havoc on his life, so he had to get treatment from a psychiatrist and therapist during that time. At the end of his first year in the program, his department told him he was not performing well in the program and would need to prove the next semester that he would be able to continue by performing at a high standard. Timothy decided to leave the program with a master's degree. Suddenly, thrust into the unknown, he had to take a job as an ESL teacher in a private language school in Washington DC. But during that time, he was able to develop a passion for ESL teaching, and he wanted to travel the world. So, he got a TEFL certificate from the Language House in Washington. He also tried to get a TESOL master's degree to get further qualification. Because Timothy wanted to become a professor, he wanted to get a job at a university. With his amazing qualifications, he could get a job at a university in China. Timothy continued to have mood swings and had some depressive episodes. But he never returned to having manic episodes. There was no relapse.

How did he accomplish this? He was continuing his medical regime religiously. He continued to take lithium, the gold standard for manic phase treatments. He used it as a long-term treatment. He also took lamotrigine to help with his anxiety. In addition to his medical regime, he ran laps around the track in his neighborhood, which boosted his endorphins and gave him a good mood. He was able to have regular appointments with his doctor. With all these continuous treatments, he was able to thrive even though he had a bipolar diagnosis. Although he continued to have mood swings, they never reached the level of manic or depressive episodes. Because he continued to monitor the state of his health, he was able to stay well for a long time.

Why was he successful? Timothy was successful because he developed a support system, which consisted of his professors, mentors, parents, friends, and doctors. He could not do all things by himself. He had to rely on others. Timothy also had a belief that God would help him through this time and lead him to the place where he needed to be. He prayed all the time that God would deliver him from his troubles, and he saw results from it. So, Timothy's story is an example of a great bipolar success story.

Looking at Timothy's story, you can see that all things are possible. Even though the odds could have been stacked against him, he was able to defeat them. He was able to accomplish his life goals, although he was suffering from bipolar disorder through this time. But he was also able to develop a program that clearly had positive results. And it was the result of hard work and dedication. It didn't happen without intentional effort. But Timothy's story can be yours too.

www.ingramcontent.com/pod-product-compliance
Lightning Source LLC
Chambersburg PA
CBHW071827080526
44589CB00012B/943